Aircraft for the Royal Air Force

by the same author

2 Group R.A.F.
The Stirling Bomber

with C. Martin Sharp
Mosquito

The Shetland, photographed by Charles Brown (photo: R.A.F. Museum)

Aircraft for the Royal Air Force

MICHAEL J. F. BOWYER

FABER AND FABER
London · Boston

First published in 1980
by Faber and Faber Limited
3 Queen Square London WC1N 3AU
Printed in Great Britain by
BAS Printers Limited
Over Wallop, Hampshire

© *Michael J. F. Bowyer 1980*

British Library Cataloguing in Publication Data

Bowyer, Michael John Frederick
Aircraft for the Royal Air Force.
1. World War, 1939–1945—Aerial operations,
British
2. Albemarle (Bomber)
3. Spitfire (Fighter planes)
4. Shetland (Seaplane)
I. Title
940.54′49′41   D786

ISBN 0-571-11515-2

Contents

Illustrations

Diagrams

Abbreviations

A. & A.E.E.	Aeroplane & Armament Experimental Establishment
A.C.A.S.(T)	Assistant Chief of the Air Staff (Training)
A.F.D.U.	Air Fighting Development Unit
A.F.E.E.	Airborne Forces Experimental Establishment
A.M.P.G.	Air Miles per Gallon
A.P.U.	Auxiliary Power Unit
A.S.R.	Air/Sea Rescue
A.S.V.	Air-to-Surface Vessel radar
B.D.U.	Bombing Development Unit
B.O.A.C.	British Overseas Airways Corporation
C.F.E.	Central Fighter Establishment
c.g.	centre of gravity
C.R.D.	Chief of Research and Development
E.A.A.S.	Empire Air Armament School
F.S.	Full Supercharger
F.T.R.	Failed to return from operations
I.A.S.	Indicated Air Speed
M.A.E.E.	Marine Aircraft Experimental Establishment
M.A.P.	Ministry of Aircraft Production
M.S.	Medium Supercharger
O.T.U.	Operational Training Unit
P.R.U.	Photographic Reconnaissance Unit
R&D	Research and Development
R.R.	Rolls-Royce
T.A.S.	True Air Speed
T.D.U.	Torpedo Development Unit

Introduction

The purpose of this book, and any which might follow to the same pattern, is to examine in detail the histories of several types of aeroplanes which were built for the Royal Air Force. They are types which played an interesting part either in Service or strategic thinking, or in the general development of aircraft. This volume considers the first Griffon-engined Spitfire (the little known Mk. XII), the Armstrong Whitworth Albemarle bomber and finally the Short Shetland flying-boat, the story of which cannot properly be told without fitting it into the overall context of British wartime flying-boat development.

Visit an air display nowadays and when a Spitfire appears such remains its attraction that thousands of cameras point towards what is, without doubt, the world's most famous aeroplane. Odds are that it whistles by to the sweet sound of a Merlin engine. If not, then it must be to the entirely different chatter-cum-growl of a Rolls-Royce Griffon.

Spitfire and Merlin have become inseparably etched into history. Rightly or wrongly, the popular impression is that they won the Battle of Britain for us. The continuing success of the combination made a new partnership—still from the Rolls-Royce stable—seem almost superfluous. But by 1944 the Spitfire–Merlin team was becoming dated, although many such machines were to continue in service for many years.

The refined Griffon Spitfires have tended to be overlooked in post-war commentary, partly because their use for aerial combat was limited and also because they mostly belong to the less exciting post-war scene. This volume firstly gives consideration to the Spitfire Mk. XII, the first Griffon version to enter service. It was a hybrid Spitfire, for its airframe was that of the Mk. V, itself little changed from that of early Spitfires. The Griffon engine was very powerful and, at the time of its birth, this Spitfire was the most brilliant of its breed. It was, however, rushed into service to meet a specific need and with a power plant which gave its best at low and medium heights. Thus, the use of the Mk. XII became limited. Only a handful were built. Therefore, their exploits can be more easily related than would be the case with versions produced in great numbers. For the first time in any volume one mark of Spitfire is studied in depth.

My second choice of subject is the Armstrong Whitworth Albemarle. It would be almost impossible to find two aeroplanes in greater contrast than the Albemarle and the Spitfire. For me the Albemarle was a daily sight between 1942 and the end of the war, for the Civilian Repair Organization handling them was Marshall of

Cambridge. To that airfield Albemarles came in plenty, their variations in detail and markings as diverse as any enthusiast could wish for—and few escaped my scrutiny. I must admit to a personal interest in the aircraft.

Whereas the Spitfire was enshrined in universal popularity the Albemarle was shunned, unwanted. This was not because it was a failure. Indeed, its performance was as forecast. However, its time scale slipped and when it eventually became available it was no better than other aircraft which had been in service for some time. The Air Staff had never expressed any wish to have it: the Albemarle was the product of Air Ministry officials. Believing there could be a shortage of strategic materials in time of war they set about providing a bomber constructed from other materials. It was a sound idea wrongly applied, for when the notion was properly utilized, the de Havilland Mosquito was the outcome. Indeed, the Mosquito owed quite a lot, from the production point of view, to the Albemarle. By the time the Albemarle was available the question was 'What can we do with it?' It answered no particular need, but the paucity of British transport aircraft and glider tugs was such that it usefully filled a gap and commendably performed during the Sicilian campaign, in the Normandy landings and over Arnhem.

Finally, the British wartime flying-boat story is featured. Again, I must admit a personal interest, for the many days which I spent watching the flying-boats at Felixstowe before the war are something I shall always cherish. The story told here revolves around the search for something better than the Sunderland. It threw up magnificent-looking machines and novel designs, but the Sunderland was just too good to be replaced. From the desire to better it came a belief that if flying-boat development was allowed to cease then Britain would suffer after the war when transports would be needed. Thus, from the wish to replace the Sunderland emerged the giant Short Shetland, the story of which is indeed a fascinating one. Frustrated in their efforts, Saunders-Roe gradually developed their design for a military aircraft into giant flying-boats for the post-war scene, this culminating in their magnificent Princess. The civil designs lie beyond the scope of this volume, but there must be some consideration of this aspect for it played a part in the story.

In the case of the Spitfire XII section I am much indebted to Wg. Cdr. H. R. Chapman, one-time Commanding Officer of No. 41 Squadron which was under his leadership in 1944. As with the other sections of this book I have drawn widely upon source material. The Operations Record Books detailing the activities of Nos. 41 and 91 Squadrons may be seen in the Public Record Office, Kew. These are to be found now in the class AIR 27, although most of my research into the Griffon Spitfire was made long ago when these records were still at the Air Historical Branch, MoD. Further references to the Spitfire XII may be found in AIR 2, AIR 10, and AVIA 18. Performance and handling data were the subject of A. & A.E.E. report /692.o. Some details of the Rolls-Royce Griffon may be found in *Flight* of 20 September 1945, but for the most part details of the Griffon are very widely scattered in published works.

In the case of the Albemarle, the son of the late Major J. Lloyd, designer of the machine, had discussed the aircraft with his father and kindly forwarded some most useful material to me. Before his untimely death, my close friend Donald Mee—who worked for some time at Baginton—gathered some material on the Albemarle and I have been able to draw from that. Some years ago Mr. Hugh Burroughes, who headed Hawkesley, very kindly read my original draft, and was able to gain for me the assistance of Mr. C. F. Joy, who looked after the wartime development of the Albemarle. As regards existing official material, the Forms 540/541 (Operations Record Books) of the relevant squadrons are now held at the Public Record Office. In addition there are references to the Albemarle in AIR 2 and AVIA 18. Articles dealing with the Albemarle may be found in the issue of *Flight* for 27 January 1944 and in *The Aeroplane* dated 30 June 1944.

In the case of the Shetland, official records are now held at the Public Record Office within Classes AIR 20 and AVIA 15. The use of material from these and the other records forementioned, and which is Crown Copyright, is acknowledged. A number of issues of *Flight* and *The Aeroplane* during the late spring and summer of 1945 carry useful features concerning the Shetland.

I am particularly indebted to Mr. C. S. Taylor, C.Eng., M.I.Mech.E., of the British Hovercraft Corporation Ltd. for his very generous help in obtaining for me numerous general arrangement drawings, reproduced in this book, of Saunders-Roe designs. These drawings are reproduced by kind permission of the British Hovercraft Corporation Ltd., in whom copyright in the original drawings is now vested.

To the Imperial War Museum I am indebted for assistance with photographs, and also to the manufacturers of the Spitfire XII and the Albemarle, although neither concern is now in existence.

Shortly before this volume was completed, the RAF Museum acquired the photograph collection of that great aviation photographer, Charles E. Brown, FRPS. I am indebted to the RAF Museum, to Mr. R. W. Mack—and indeed Charles E. Brown—for some beautiful photographs of the Shetland.

Cambridge
April 1980   MICHAEL J. F. BOWYER

Part One

The Supermarine Spitfire XII:
The First with the Griffon

Rolls-Royce Merlin and the Supermarine Spitfire are inseparable, evocative names, symbolic of Britain and British quality. It was a combination which might well be considered our greatest single contribution to victory in the 1939–45 war.

The Merlin was the most efficient engine in a skilfully developed line, and by 1939 development had resulted in a power plant, which—with repeated modification and refinement—would become suitable for aircraft far in advance of any envisaged when the war broke out. Its output was only one of its features; small frontal area and high power/weight ratio, added to amazing reliability, made the Merlin a winner throughout its long career.

Before hostilities broke out, Rolls-Royce wondered how long the Merlin could maintain its superiority, and whether it would remain suitable for advanced combat aircraft for many years. Guarding against possible inadequacy—which never arose—Rolls-Royce looked to an entirely new engine similar in size to the Merlin yet not based upon it. This became the Rolls-Royce Griffon.

The company had produced a high-performance engine, the Type 'R', for the 1929–31 Schneider Trophy Supermarine racers, after which the Royal Navy showed interest in a de-rated version for a torpedo bomber. Planning of that engine did commence, but was soon abandoned as work became concentrated on the engine which was to become the Merlin. However, naval interest in a Type 'R' successor was renewed in 1938. This new engine was bench run that year and formed the basis of the Griffon. Initially it was known as the Rolls-Royce RR-37 Vee-12, as the company was continuing its line of twelve-cylinder 60° upright-Vee liquid-cooled in-line engines. The cylinder arrangement and engine dimensions resembled those of the Rolls-Royce 'R', and the Griffon's crankshaft design was based upon research for the post-Schneider engine.

One requirement of the new power plant was that it must be easily installed in existing Merlin-engined designs. A frontal area of 7·9 sq. ft. had been achieved, against the Merlin's 7·5 sq. ft., and the new engine looked likely to ensure a steady improvement in fighter performance. Yet so successful was the Merlin that, although the decision to proceed with Griffon production was taken in September 1939, it was not until mid-1942 that the new engine was ready. Flight trials commenced in 1940 when a Hawker Henley test-bed, L3414, began flying.

The Griffon was in no sense a scaled-up Merlin, although it had some similar features; it arose from a desire to redesign the Merlin, eliminate some snags, increase capacity and yet retain the smallest overall dimensions. Swept volume was about one third greater, which was made possible by increasing the cylinder bore to the same size as in the Rolls-Royce 'R'. The Griffon was 23 per cent larger than the Merlin. One respect in which it differed from the Merlin was that it had a remote gearbox shaft drive from the engine, upon which were mounted the mechanically driven accessories needed to operate such features as undercarriage retraction, wheel brakes, wing flaps, blind-flying panel and dario generator. New features were the cam and duplex magneto drives from the front of the engine to relieve valve operation from as much variation as possible. The crankshaft speed was greatly reduced in transmission to the camshaft, which gave fairly constant propeller revolutions, and front drive reduced the engine length. The main bearings and big ends were lubricated from the hollow interior of the camshaft. A new engine mounting was devised, built up from a tubular structure to a semi-cantilever-type mounting fabricated from light alloy extrusion and sheeting.

The main aim in the minds of the Rolls-Royce team was to apply the Griffon to the Spitfire. There was now close liaison with Supermarine who were also looking at ways to improve their fighter. During the early weeks of the war Rolls-Royce schemed the Griffon to fit the existing Spitfire airframe when the engines became available. The power output was assessed as 1,735 h.p.

Air Ministry staff viewed this machine as a long term project, and compared it with the planned Spitfire II. Their remarkably accurate calculations suggested a strengthened airframe some 800–900 lb. heavier than that of the Spitfire Mk. 1, an all-up weight of 7,100 lb., a top speed of 393 m.p.h. at 18,500 ft., climb rate of 5·1 minutes to 15,000 ft., an endurance on 84 gallons of fuel of about 15 minutes less than the Spitfire 1s and a landing run of 600 yd. It seemed likely it would need larger tyres and a 100 lb. compensating weight in the rear fuselage. These initial calculations were soon altered due to some errors, and the top speed was raised to a likely 401 m.p.h. at 18,500 ft.

The decision to hold the scheme for a Griffon Spitfire was taken on 15 November 1939. Such a radical alteration to the successful Spitfire prompted the question of heavier calibre guns. On 13 December 1939 discussion ranged around four 20mm Hispano cannon—drum or belt fed—and alternatively arrangements of .303 in. Browning guns or six .50 in. American machine guns upon which preference finally fell.

Hawker Aircraft were interested in applying the Griffon to the Hurricane—very optimistically so, for figures showed a performance much superior to that of the Griffon Spitfire. Some of these makers' figures are given below.

	Hawker Griffon Hurricane	*Supermarine Griffon Spitfire*
Maximum speed at 18,500 ft.	421 m.p.h.	411 m.p.h.
Economic endurance	2 hours	1·75 hours
Take-off run	470 yd.	350 yd.

1. The prototype Spitfire III late in 1940 by which time standard wing tips had again been fitted

Realizing that the Griffon would not be available or needed for some time, Supermarine concentrated on wedding the 1,390 h.p. Merlin XX to the Spitfire, thereby producing the first major development feature in that aeroplane's career. This new version was designated Spitfire Mk. III, and it has a niche in the Spitfire XII story.

In its original configuration the Type 330 Spitfire III differed little from its predecessors. A Merlin XX drove a three-bladed 10 ft. 9 in. diameter Rotol constant speed propeller. The Mk. III had an all-up weight of 6,650 lb. against the 6,050 lb. of the Spitfire I.

During March 1940 the prototype Mk. III N3297 was first flown and was followed by a second example, N3171. Handling trials of the latter showed it to have a top speed of 320·5 m.p.h. at 10,000 ft. (reached in 3·5 min.), 353·5 m.p.h. at 20,000 ft. (attained in 7·7 min.) and 319 m.p.h. at 30,000 ft. (to which height it climbed in 16·4 min.). The take-off run was 225 yd., service ceiling 34,700 ft. Its best rate of climb was 2,905 f.p.m. at 11,000 ft. (reached in 3·9 min.). It was faster on the climb than the Spitfire II but little better in other respects.

Supermarine then turned their attention to improving handling qualities, particularly the rate of roll. They decided to clip the wing tips, reducing the wing area to 220 sq. ft. and the wing span to 30 ft. 6 in. It was this feature that was going to link the Mk. III to the Griffon-engined Mk. XII.

Tests with the clipped-wing Mk. III were carried out in July 1940 with the aircraft's weight still about 6,600 lb. Take-off and landing runs were much increased, taking it 405 yd. to unstick and 605 yd. to climb to 50 ft. The braked landing run was 600 yd. Comparative figures for the Spitfire I (Merlin III) were: (a) with out-dated wooden propeller at 5,800 lb. weight, 420 yd. for take off, 720 yd. to climb to 50 ft. and landing run 380 yd.; (b) with Rotol constant speed propeller at 6,050 lb. weight, 225 yd. for take off, 370 yd. to climb to 50 ft. and braked landing run of 310 yd. It was the field performance more than anything else which was disturbing.

To Air Marshal Sir Hugh Dowding, Commander-in-Chief, Fighter Command, the landing run of the Mk. II (clipped) was 'dangerously long'. He prohibited its use for night fighting. In addition, the square wing tips made it resemble the Messerschmitt Bf 109E and a case of mistaken identity had occurred by August 1940. Dowding asked whether the production Mk. III could have conventional wing tips to reduce the landing run. He was worried, too, that the wing-loading of a clipped wing Spitfire would be too high, for that of the Spitfire I was reckoned as maximum for its structure. 'If we add extra weight to the Spitfire,' he argued, 'we surely should increase the wing area.'

On 21 August 1940 a meeting was held with the Assistant Chief of the Air Staff (Training) to discuss the Spitfire III. Clipped wing tips improved control, but they reduced performance at higher altitudes. Stronger spars would allow for increased wing-loading. Just how much strengthening was needed would be decided upon after further tests. As a result of these came the later decision to fit long-span wings to improve high-altitude performance.

An order for 1,000 Mk. IIIs with conventional wing tips was placed on 24 October 1940, but other events were by then overtaking the first new variant. The most important of these was the installation of the Merlin XLV in the Mk. I/II airframe to produce the Spitfire V.

Autumn 1940 found Supermarine still pondering upon a Griffon Spitfire's likely performance. Only by placing fairing blisters over its cylinder banks could the Griffon be installed. Castle Bromwich's management wrote to the Ministry of Aircraft Production on 12 November 1940 stating that: 'We have been working on an advanced version of the Spitfire with a Griffon engine. This we call the Mk. IV. We discussed this in January last with Sir Wilfrid Freeman, and he gave verbal instructions to proceed with two prototypes. Work is proceeding, but we have no contract.'

The success of the Spitfire V (Merlin XLV) was soon apparent. Plans for the Mk. III were cancelled and the way ahead cleared for the Griffon Spitfire. Air Staff interest was renewed and in February 1941 they asked Supermarine for their latest ideas for such an aircraft. The company passed them to the Director of Operational Requirements, Air Commodore R. B. Mansell, on 27 February 1941.

Hawkers were still hopeful that a Griffon Hurricane might emerge, but their '370 m.p.h. plus' suggestion was considered not advanced enough whereas, in the words of the Air Staff, the Spitfire was 'a natural and practical development which will give a fighter with a top speed of 400–410 m.p.h. at 23,000 ft., and a ceiling of 36,000/37,000 ft. which gives the Spitfire a new lease of life.' Supermarine confidence that the R.A.F. would require such a machine was

2.   The Spitfire III with clipped wing tips

sufficient for them to start building parts in February 1941 although they still awaited a contract.

Investigations had suggested that such an aircraft could have a top speed as high as 430 m.p.h. at around 23,000 ft. and a service ceiling of 38,500 ft. Griffon development was expected to follow the lines of the Merlin, thus incorporating intercoolers and two-stage blowers for extra power so that eventually a Griffon Spitfire might be expected to reach 470 m.p.h. at 35,000 ft. and have an operational ceiling of 46,300 ft. These figures were proved to be too optimistic, the definitive Spitfire eventually achieving a speed of around 450 m.p.h.

Supermarine stated that modifications needed to the existing Spitfire 'B' airframe would not be all that great. The engine mounting would need to be changed and the cowling redesigned. The existing engine bulkhead could be retained, also engine attachment points. The engine fuel and cooling systems would need some alterations and the radiator would need to be enlarged. Fuselage length would increase by 5–6 inches, and the tailwheel would be retractable as on the Spitfire III. Minor strengthening of the wing spar would be needed, provision being made for fuel tanks to carry 35 gallons in the wing leading edges. Larger tyres of up to 53 lb./sq. in. and a longer undercarriage chassis by 7 in. seemed necessary, along with modifications to the wing ribs allowing six cannon to be installed. Wing-loading would be about 32 lb./sq. ft., and larger new-type slotted flaps should ensure a landing run well within acceptable limits. To allow for the highest possible ceiling, wing tips of increased span would be available, remaining interchangeable with the normal tips, the greater span extending to 40 ft. 6 in. giving a wing area of 250 sq. ft. These figures were based upon deliberations which followed the clipping of the Mk. III's wings. Duration would be increased by having 130 gal. internal tankage. For very high-altitude flying a pressure cabin might be installed.

Supermarine provided details of two versions of a Griffon Spitfire, as shown in the following table.

	2 × 20 mm. cannon (120 r.p.g.) 4 × .303 in. machine guns (350 r.p.g.)	4 × 20 mm. cannon (120 r.p.g.)
Weight bare (lb.)	5,571	5,571
Armour (lb.)	189	189
Fixed load (lb.)	250	250
Tare weight (lb.)	6,010	6,010
Removable load (lb.)	1,000	1,200
Fuel—110 gal. (lb.)	795	795
Oil—10 gal. (lb.)	90	90
Weight loaded (lb.)	7,895	8,095
Maximum speeds (m.p.h.):		
25,000 ft.	433	429
15,000 ft.	388	374
Take-off run (yd.)	275	285
Take-off run over 50 ft. (yd.)	405	425
Time to 15,000 ft. (min.)	5·3	5·5
Time to 35,000 ft. (min.)	13·3	13·9
Operational ceiling (ft.)	35,400	33,800
Landing run over 50 ft. (yd.)	575	595

The suggested engine was the Griffon RG 25M for which engine powers and settings would be:

'M' blower: take off, 1,640 b.h.p. at 3,000 revs. 5,500 ft., 1,550 b.h.p. at 2,600 revs.

'S' blower: 16,000 ft., 1,430 b.h.p. at 2,600 revs.

Max. b.h.p.: 'M' 5,000 ft., 1,610 b.h.p. at 2,650 revs.
'S' 19,000 ft., 1,425 b.h.p. at 2,750 revs.

Propeller: Four-bladed Rotol constant speed to absorb the greater power.

On 15 March 1941 the Commander-in-Chief, Fighter Command, having heard that the Griffon Spitfire was being revived, requested details from Air Ministry. In response, Air Commodore R. B. Mansell replied on 24 March with an estimate of the likely capabilities of such an aeroplane. They considered that its normal weight would be 8,000 lb., they toned down the makers' estimate of maximum speed to about 410 m.p.h. at 22,500 ft. and suggested a cruising speed in 'M' gear of about 292 m.p.h. at 20,000 ft., 340 m.p.h. at 20,000 ft. in 'S' gear. It would take 7·6 min. to reach 20,000 ft. and have a service ceiling of 36,500 ft. Supermarine had suggested 38,500 ft. for the mixed armament version and 37,900 ft. for the four-cannon variant. Endurance would be about two and a half hours at 210 m.p.h. plus 15 min. for take off and the same period at maximum speed. Universal wings would allow for an alternative armament of four 20 mm. cannon, or two 20 mm. cannon and four ·303 in. machine guns or eight machine guns of ·303 in. calibre. Fuel load would be 130 gal.

At high altitude the aircraft should have performed slightly better than the Hawker Typhoon, the latter being expected to have superior performance to 35,000 ft., above which the Griffon Spitfire would be superior. At 22,000 ft., it should have reached 410 m.p.h. compared with the Typhoon's estimated speed of 420 m.p.h. In reality the Typhoon reached its maximum speed of 405 m.p.h. at 18,000 ft., had a service ceiling of 33,000 ft., took 6·3 min. to climb to 15,000 ft. and 7·6 min. to reach 20,000 ft.

During March and April 1941 the Air Staff and Air Ministry consulted one another, compiling a specification to submit to Vickers-Supermarine for the Spitfire IV (Griffon) and met on 20 March to discuss a draft. This was then talked over with the manufacturers and on 19 April 1941 a firm contract for two prototypes was finally placed. Supermarine considered it possible to build a prototype by August 1941 and put the variant into production during December 1941. It was estimated that Rolls-Royce could commence Griffon production in time for deliveries to commence in March 1942.

Air Marshal Sir W. Sholto Douglas, Commander-in-Chief, Fighter Command, was unhappy about the projected armament, arguing that it would be no better than that of the Spitfires II and V. He suggested twelve ·303 in. guns with 350 r.p.g. or two 20 mm. cannon and six ·303 in. guns, or four 20 mm. cannon. However, with the planned wing fuel tankage there was insufficient room for six machine guns in each mainplane. Supermarine's Chief Designer, Mr. J. Smith, suggested six cannon but this meant much reduced ammunition. Lord Beaverbrook, head of M.A.P., urged caution and suggested waiting to see how the Hurricane fared with twelve ·303 in. guns, but Air Marshal Sholto Douglas repeated his desire for the armament that he had suggested and this was placed in the specification.

On 23 May 1941 Specification F. 4/41 was issued to Supermarine for the single-seat Spitfire IV, derived from earlier Spitfires and employing their standard components. It was to be suitable for world-wide operations. Maximum speed should be not less than 410 m.p.h. at 22,000 ft., and fuel load should allow for 45 min. at maximum power, three and a half hours at maximum economical speed at 20,000 ft. (for patrol) and 15 min. at maximum speed in level flight for combat. There would be increased endurance for operational and reinforcement flights employing auxiliary tanks. Additional fuel would also be needed for 15 min. at maximum power for level flight at 20,000 ft. The take off to clear 50 ft. would be 500 yd., and the landing run over 50 ft. about 700 yd. Universal armament was now to allow for six 20 mm. cannon, or two 20 mm. cannon and eight machine guns, or twelve ·303 in. machine guns, and the heated guns must be easily removable. The gun-sight could be a reflector or prismatic type and the cockpit would be armoured against ·303 in. fire from 100 yd. The windscreen, 1·5 in. thick, should be bullet-proofed. No large alterations in trim would be needed, and the aircraft would have night-flying equipment. Just how well Supermarine met these requirements will become evident.

The Spitfire IV, the first entirely new prototype Spitfire airframe so far ordered, went ahead to F. 4/41. Two experimental Griffon Spitfire airframes were ordered—DP845 and DP851 (the latter became a development prototype for later versions of the Griffon Spitfire, discussion of which lies outside the range of this book). An order for 750 production Mk. IVs was placed on 23 August 1941.

Minor alterations to the specification were made in September 1941. Maximum speed had now to be 410 m.p.h. at 23,000 ft. The fuel load would allow for $2\frac{1}{4}$ hours' flying at economical speed at 20,000 ft. for patrol, service ceiling would be 39,000 ft. plus, take-off run with operational load would not exceed 500 yd. and landing run 700 yd. Armament could now comprise six 20 mm. cannon, or two 20 mm. cannon and four ·50 in. machine guns.

Wing span of DP845 was conventionally set at 36 ft. 10 in. and the length at 31 ft. 10 in. An enlarged rudder area was agreed as this would counteract increased torque from the more powerful engine.

Supermarine Type 337, Spitfire IV prototype DP845, first flew in December 1941 powered by a Griffon II. The airframe stemmed from an amalgamation of features of the Spitfire III and Mk. Vc. Another variant of the Spitfire was already in service, the P.R. Mk. V Type 'D'. To avoid duplication of mark numbers and ensure numerical continuity of versions in service this reconnaissance version was redesignated Mk. IV and, to provide space for future Merlin developments, DP845 became the Spitfire XII (prototype). DP851 became the Mk. XX from which came an advanced family of Griffon Spitfires.

Testing the Mk. XII

Flight testing of DP845 went ahead during 1942. Refinements were incorporated and the engine subjected to a variety of trials. A mock-up of the six-cannon armament which the specification included was fitted, but rejected due to its weight. However, it was for a very different reason that the future of the Spitfire XII was radically altered. In June 1942, Fw 190 fighter-bombers commenced low-level attacks on south coast towns. These pernicious aircraft flew low across the Channel below the cover of British defensive radar making interception extremely difficult other than by flying costly defensive standing patrols.

3. DP845 as the prototype Spitfire IV and fitted with six mock-up cannon.
Note the standard wing tips

4. DP845 photographed during early official trials. Normal armament has been fitted,
and the wing tips remain standard. Clearly seen is the broad chord rudder

The Typhoon had still to become fully operational and suitable defensive fighters were not yet available. So now the Spitfire XII had a different and special niche to fill. With a Griffon rated for low- and medium-level flying it was chosen for the special anti-Fw 190 task, and it was now that the useful work with the Spitfire III came into its own. The wing tips of the prototype Mk. XII were clipped to improve its rate of roll at low levels, in manner similar to that of the prototype Mk. III in the summer of 1940, and its span was reduced to 32 ft. 7 in. A call came for rapid development of the Mk. XII and in the summer of 1942, even before the prototype had undergone official trials, it was decided to produce hastily a limited number of Mk. XIIs after DP845 out-performed a captured Fw 190.

On 10 September 1942, DP845 arrived at Boscombe Down where the Aeroplane & Armament Experimental Establishment were eager to assess its capabilities as a low-level interceptor. First, its speed and climb performance were measured and there was some disappointment that it did not attain the speeds specified and expected. Trials showed the following figures.

At a take-off weight of 7,320 lb. with radiator flap open:

Maximum speeds

At sea level 346 m.p.h. T.A.S. in M.S. gear.
4,000 ft. 364 m.p.h. T.A.S. in M.S. gear.
5,700 ft. 372 m.p.h. T.A.S. in F.S. gear.
10,000 ft. 370·5 m.p.h. T.A.S. in M.S. gear.
12,000 ft. 370 m.p.h. T.A.S. in F.S. gear.
17,800 ft. Maximum speed attained, 397 m.p.h. in F.S. gear.
24,000 ft. 394 m.p.h. T.A.S. in F.S. gear.

Climb performance

2·25 min. to 8,000 ft., rate of climb 3,130 f.p.m. in M.S. gear.
6·7 min. to 20,000 ft., rate of climb 2,230 f.p.m. in F.S. gear.
12·95 min. to 30,000 ft., rate of climb, 1,110 f.p.m. in F.S. gear.
17·55 min. to 34,000 ft., rate of climb 660 f.p.m. in F.S. gear.
23·8 min. to 37,000 ft., rate of climb 320 f.p.m. in F.S. gear.

Maximum rate of climb

In M.S. gear 3,040 f.p.m. at 4,000 ft.
In M.S. gear 3,040 f.p.m. at 4,000 ft.

Service ceiling

39,000 ft.

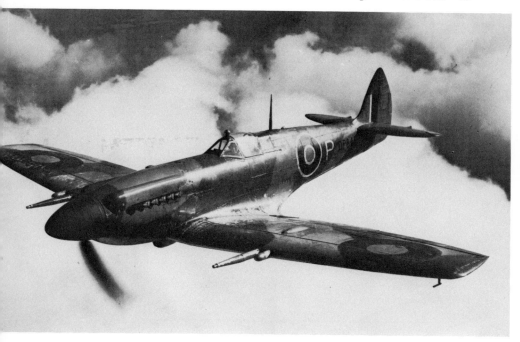

5.   DP845 in flight, after the clipping of the wing tips

The Griffon II in DP845 had a rating of 1,720 h.p. for take off, 1,730 h.p. at 750 ft. and 1,490 h.p. at 14,000 ft. The reduction gear rating was 0·45:1 and the propeller a four-bladed Rotol XH54D-RM-55. A tropical radiator and oil cooler of the type used on the Spitfire Vc were fitted. At a weight of 7,415 lb. the c.g. was 4·9 in. aft of the datum with undercarriage down. However, on climb, with the radiator open, the oil temperature was suitable for temperate summer conditions, but just failed the requirement for tropical summer operations above 31,000 ft., although level flight in rich mixture M.S. gear at 5,500 ft. and F.S. gear at 18,000 ft. (both full throttle test heights), showed acceptable oil cooling. Without some modifications this Griffon Spitfire was therefore unsuitable for overseas deployment.

Engine limitations at this time were maximum power for take off and up to 1,000 ft. for five minutes' flying using 2,750 revs. and +12 lb. sq. in. boost, level five minutes' limit at 2,750 revs. and +7 lb. sq. in. boost, maximum cruise rich mixture 2,400 revs. and +7 lb. sq. in. boost and maximum cruise weak mixture 2,400 revs. and +6 lb. sq. in. boost. For the best speed on the climb with radiator shut the supercharger gear change came at about 9,000 ft. The best normal climb speed was 190 m.p.h. I.A.S. to 16,000 ft. decreasing by 3·5 m.p.h. per 1,000 ft. thereafter. On the third test flight to assess climb performance supercharger gear was changed to F.S. at 11,000 ft. for optimum climb but normally combat rating restricted this to five minutes' use.

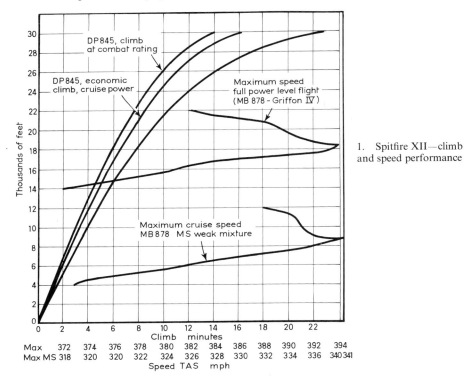

1.   Spitfire XII—climb and speed performance

At low engine speeds the Griffon was found to surge. Main carburettor jets of 0·345 in. diameter were then replaced by others of 0·355 in. diameter and the test programme repeated. The engine had individual ejector stub exhausts. During this phase DP845 mounted two 20 mm. cannon and four ·303 in. machine guns.

External flush-riveted finish was non-standard. There was filling at joints and edges of overlapping panels, and the entire aircraft surface was smoothly polished. Fuel tanks carried 95 gallons but production derivatives would disappointingly carry only 85 gallons since their fuel system was that of the Spitfire V. Thus, the duration of flight forecast for the Griffon Spitfire using 5–6 a.m.p.g. would be considerably less than specified. Take-off weight would be lower in production aircraft than the 7,415 lb. of DP845 since they carried less fuel and had a lower tare weight. Service weight of the production Mk. XII came out at around 7,390 lb.

Handling trials showed the Griffon Spitfire similar to other variants except in one important respect. The propeller on the Griffon version rotated in the opposite direction to that of Merlin Spitfires, and the broad chord rudder also brought slight handling changes. With the propeller as fitted to DP845 the c.g. range was over the position 4·2 in. to 4·9 in. aft of datum, but with Hydulignum propeller these positions were assessed as about 0·3 in. further aft. The ground view over the nose was little changed, and more powerful brakes were fitted.

On take off the prototype would quickly swing to the right, a large swing developing if the engine was opened rapidly. This occurred markedly in the early parts of the run, and the rudder proved insufficiently powerful to check the trouble despite its additional area. Some directional control was therefore lost, the amount depending upon the speed as the engine opened up. The rudder was heavy when full movement was applied, and full left trim was needed at take off. Reduced boost did little to alleviate the problem.

In flight, the aircraft handled similarly to the Spitfire V, but rudder control was heavy and the constant trimming needed was a feature at variance with the specification. Longitudinally the Mk. XII was more positive than the Spitfire V due to its c.g. being further forward. There was no reduction in manoeuvrability but aileron forces and movements were greater. The stalling speed, flaps and undercarriage down was 75 m.p.h. I.A.S. and with flaps and undercarriage up was 65 m.p.h. I.A.S. Dives to 450 m.p.h. were satisfactory. Under most conditions there was noticeable vibration from the engine, and fuel consumption trials indicated still air ranges of about 400 air miles in M.S. gear at 5,000 ft., 425 air miles in F.S. gear at 20,000 ft. and 420 air miles in F.S. gear at 30,000 ft.

The main criticism of the Mk. XII prototype was that the rudder should have been lightened before its area was increased, but to speed production it was decided to let the aircraft go forward with the existing fitting. With few modifications the Spitfire XII was acceptable for front-line service.

Into production

In the summer of 1942 the production version of the Griffon IIB (which had powered DP845), the Griffon III, entered production. The run was short, for only 100 were to be built. Like its predecessor, the Griffon III had a reduction gear ratio of 0·451:1 whereas a successor for a handful of Spitfire XIIs, the Mk. IV, featured a gear reduction ratio of 0·510:1. Only twenty-five such engines were manufactured.

The Griffon III wedded to the Spitfire Vc airframe, the wings of which were clipped in Spitfire III fashion, resulted in the Spitfire L.F. XII. The first forty-five examples EN221–EN238 and EN601–EN627 were within a batch of 500 Spitfires ordered from Vickers-Armstrong's (Supermarine) main works in August 1941, most of which were completed as Merlin-engined Mk. IXs. Initial production was slow, the first of the five aircraft completed in 1942 not being flown until October of that year. This machine, EN221, was set aside for acceptance trials and proceeded to A. & A.E.E., Boscombe Down, early in November 1942. A month later it was joined by the second built, EN222. These were compared with the prototype.

The third machine, EN223, flown in November 1942, was despatched to the Air Fighting Development Unit, Duxford, for tactical assessment, arriving on the station shortly before Christmas 1942. Makers' test-flying continued, using DP845 and, from December 1942, EN224. By early 1943 it was possible to summarize the attainments of the production Mk. XII and compare it with other versions of the Spitfire.

Although the Mk. XII was developed from the 'B' airframe it included features from later Spitfire designs. EN221–EN238 and EN601–EN627 were sandwiched on the production lines between Mk. IXs, inheriting features from them such as fixed tailwheels. Later airframes from the same source were taken from batches of Mk. VIII production, this version having a retractable tailwheel, an item featured by Spitfire XIIs MB794–MB805, MB829–MB863 and MB875–MB882.

EN223 tested at Duxford at the end of 1942 had an all-up weight of 7,400 lb. and, fitted with a wooden propeller, had a maximum speed of 372 m.p.h. at 5,700 ft. and 397 m.p.h. at 18,000 ft. These figures equated those of the polished prototype, but the engine ran rough and there was much criticism of the take-off qualities. It was the considered opinion of Duxford's pilots that the Mk. XII would quickly get out of control on take off if a pilot did not respond rapidly to situations arising. To counteract the troubles, modifications were made to the propeller pitch settings. The first six Mk. XIIs had Dural propellers, the remainder wooden propellers and the latter afforded some improvement in handling.

Two fuel tanks were sited one above the other in the fuselage forward of the cockpit, the upper tank holding 48 gallons and the lower tank 37 gallons in the case of EN-serialled aircraft, as with the Mk. IX. The MB-serialled machines also had two fuel tanks, with 36 gallons in the upper and 49 gallons in the lower tank. In the first seven Mk. XIIs the oil tank was positioned behind the pilot, which was quite unacceptable. Subsequent machines had it placed ahead of the fireproof bulkhead at the rear of the engine. There was provision for a 30-gallon (later 90-gallon) jettisonable fuel tank, but it was some time before any were carried on the Mk. XIIs.

Initial trials were with Griffon III machines, but a retro-fit was made of a Griffon IV in EN222 which was then fitted with a Dural propeller for comparison with EN223, which retained a Griffon III and had a wooden propeller. The only major difference with the Griffon IV was in the rate of climb, which increased by 600 f.p.m., reducing time to 10,000 ft. by 30 sec. With the Griffon III the initial rate of climb was faster for the first 1,000 ft. after which the Griffon IV machine climbed away, this being noticeable from 3,000–4,000 ft. At 10,000 ft. it had about a 25 sec. lead. Such gains would be important for combating low-flying Fw 190s. At sea level the maximum speed of the Spitfire XII was about 345 m.p.h., making it slightly slower than an average Fw 190, which attained about 350 m.p.h. and had an initial climb rate of about 2,200 f.p.m.

The Griffon-IV-engined aircraft proved slightly slower in level flight, and its climb rate equalled the Merlin-powered Mk. IX to 4,000 ft., after which it was inferior. By way of comparison, the Mk. IX in unclipped-wing form and medium-altitude engine rating had a top speed of about 312 m.p.h. at sea level in M.S. gear and 403 m.p.h. at 27,400 ft. in F.S. gear. The improved view over the nose of the Mk. XII would have made it a better fighter-bomber than the Merlin-engined Spitfires. Comparison with the Mk. IX (Merlin 66) showed the Mk. XII

6.   EN223, the third production Spitfire XII, photographed at the Air Fighting Development Unit on 4 April 1943. This aircraft joined 91 Squadron in November 1943 and was struck off charge following a battle accident in January 1944

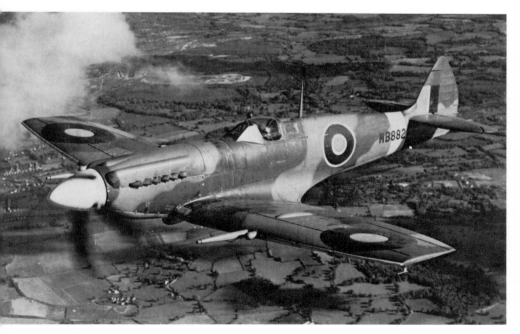

7.   Spitfire XII MB882 (Griffon IV) was initially delivered to 33 M.U. on 24 November 1943 and served with 41 Squadron between December 1943 and September 1944. It then spent a short time at the Fighter Leaders' School, Milfield

faster at sea level by about 10 m.p.h. By 10,000 ft. it was slower by about 9 m.p.h. and this speed fell away to 15,000 ft., beyond which it proved slightly faster to 19,000 ft. where speed fell away again. There was not the slightest doubt that the Mk. XII would have a fairly specialized role in low- and medium-level actions.

As regards its likely adversary, the Fw 190A-3 currently in use had a maximum speed of about 385 m.p.h. at 19,000 ft., a service ceiling of 36,000 ft. and could climb to 18,000 ft. in 6·5 min.

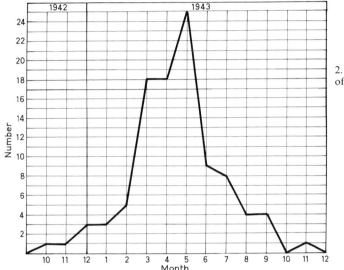

2.   Production deliveries of Spitfire Mk. XII

On 11 January 1943 the first example of the Mk. XII to reach a maintenance unit arrived at No. 5 M.U. to be equipped for front-line service. However, by this time interest in the Griffon Spitfire had been aroused in naval quarters, particularly as the Navy already had experience of the engine with the forthcoming Firefly. They wished to know the Spitfire XII's suitability for carrier use and modification to Seafire type. Accordingly EN227, initially delivered to 45 M.U. on 21 January 1943, was returned to Supermarine for suitable modifications before proceeding to No. 778 Squadron at Hurn on 28 February 1943. There it remained on loan until EN226 also modified joined 778 Squadron on 14 March 1943. The low-level performance impressed pilots of this service trials squadron, but the take-off swing would make carrier operation rather hazardous. Without some more aerodynamic correction, which was achieved with the Seafire XV, the naval derivative of the Mk. XII, the Griffon Spitfire was unsuitable for naval use.

Squadron service and operational career

Fourteen Mk. XIIs had been built by February 1943. Fighter Command already had plans to equip two squadrons with this version and to place them centrally on the south coast to aid Typhoon squadrons presently flying standing patrols and being held available for rapid scrambles in order to catch Fw 190 raiders.

The first squadron to be withdrawn for conversion was No. 41 using Spitfire Vbs and based at Tangmere in Sussex. There, on 24 February 1943, they took on charge their first Mk. XII, EN228, which was joined by EN233 on 28 February and EN231 on 9 March 1943. The squadron moved to High Ercall on 26 March, withdrawing to train with the new Spitfire version. By the end of March, No. 41 Squadron had nineteen Mk. XIIs, the last two machines arriving at the end of the month.

For the pilots the new type took some getting used to, but there were no major teething troubles to surmount. As soon as they had mastered the inherent swing in the design the Spitfire XII was seen to be a very efficient machine. The first firing practice took place from Valley on 30 March and the following day the squadron managed to get twelve aircraft into the air for the first time. Formation flying and battle training then took place.

Two pilots were at Valley for air-firing practice on 3 April when the Sector Operations Room gave warning that a high-level reconnaissance aircraft was proceeding northwards over the Irish Sea. EN601 and EN609 were standing by armed and refuelled, ready for more practice flying, but the chance of action was irresistible.

At 16.00 hours Flg. Off. C. R. Birbeck and Sgt. J. Stonier were ordered to intercept the raider, probably a Ju 88. It was reported to be at 27,000 feet. Both pilots searched about that level, but in vain. They landed, disappointed, at 16.35 hours with nothing to report—except that they had become the first two R.A.F. pilots to fly Griffon Spitfires on operational sorties.

The first fortnight of April passed busily as the squadron put finishing touches to operational training, then on 12–13 April No. 41 Squadron moved south to Hawkinge. Long resident at this station had been No. 91 Squadron whose main role since early 1941 had been to fly 'Jim Crows', patrols and reconnaissance flights over the Channel, mainly to observe shipping movement. On 16 April 1943 No. 41 Squadron took over this commitment and at 10.45 hours Sqn. Ldr. R. H. Harries and Flt. Lt. T. R. Poynton took off on the first operational patrol using Spitfire XIIs, for an uneventful reconnaissance in the Dieppe area. Such pairs of Spitfires became a regular early morning feature.

On the evening of 17 April 1943 the Mk. XIIs fired their guns in anger for the first time. All Mk. XIIs had the Universal Wing carrying two 20 mm. cannon and four ·303 in. Browning machine guns. Flg. Off. C. R. Birbeck strafed a small ship, but it was Flt. Lt. R. Hogarth who took the prize. Patrolling over the sea between Calais and Ostend, he unexpectedly came upon a Ju 88 which he quickly shot into the sea to become first victor with the new fighter. Current operations were mainly in the area where the Ju 88 was shot down. On 21 April Flg. Off. D. Haywood became the first pilot to shoot up ground targets, on a sortie which took him five miles into France south of Boulogne.

Early next morning Flg. Off. H. B. Moffett, R.C.A.F., was flying in the Cap Gris Nez area when he was attacked by three enemy fighters, but a fast getaway saved him. A patrol to Dieppe came on 23 April to an area where bandits had been reported, but no trace was found of them. However, Flt. Lt. T. R. Poynton in EN601 failed to return from patrol.

The first certain engagement with enemy fighters came on 27 April, when Flg. Offs. D. Haywood and C. R. Birbeck, on a reconnaissance to the Calais–Somme Estuary line, met two Fw 190s. A fast fight developed, as a result of which Birbeck shot down an Fw 190. Reconnaissances continued into May, with the squadron gaining more experience with the Mk. XIIs while No. 91 Squadron—which had retired to Honiley in Warwickshire—began conversion to Mk. XIIs, the first of which, EN613, they received on 22 April 1943. On 9 May No. 91 Squadron moved to Wittering taking seven Mk. XIIs and three Vbs, and they then spent eleven days flying their new machines, mainly from King's Cliffe, returning to Hawkinge ready for battle on 21 May. By then No. 41 Squadron had seen quite a lot of action.

On 3 May Flt. Lt. H. L. Parry and Sgt. W. L. East flew a patrol to Dieppe, in answer to which the Luftwaffe scrambled eight Fw 190s. They overpowered Sgt. East, but Parry, using his marginally superior speed, escaped to Hawkinge. At this time a great number of patrols were being flown, but the squadron was short of pilots and reckoned it needed a month to bring one to operational standard on the Mk. XII. Meanwhile, Fw 190 fighter-bombers were busily making very low flights across the Channel to attack coastal targets. Scrambles were ordered, usually too late, and no successes were achieved. On 21 May 1943 when No. 91 Squadron arrived at Hawkinge, they took over the 'Jim Crow' patrols to gain operational experience and on 25 May participated in the most exciting event so far in the Mk. XII's operational career.

Sqn. Ldr. R. H. Harries and Plt. Off. J. Round of No. 91 Squadron had just landed from a low patrol in the Hastings area with Flg. Off. J. P. Maridor and Plt. Off. D. H. Davy when a sudden scramble was ordered for the squadron at 21.50 hours. Some Fw 190s were approaching Folkestone at low level, so the four pilots who had just landed raced off to intercept, as about one dozen enemy aircraft were closing fast on the coast. On seeing the Spitfires the Fw 190s scattered. All dropped their bombs in the sea, except one, which placed a bomb in Folkestone's public swimming-pool and injured one person. Meanwhile, Flt. Lt. I. G. Matthew and Flt. Lt. N. A. Kynaston had been ordered into the air, followed by Flg. Off. G. W. Bond, who joined in the chase which had developed but was unable to catch up with the fight. Harries and his two Sections, though, had no difficulty in overtaking the Fw 190s, five of which were confirmed as shot down. Two fell to Harries, one to Maridor, one to Round. Davy scored hits on another. Bond raced across the Channel and caught up with a Fw 190 at which he fired without, he thought, scoring any hits. Suddenly the Fw 190 dived into the sea. Although the Folkestone guns had engaged the enemy, and No. 91 Squadron had flown through the fire, none of the squadron's aircraft was damaged. The action proved that, given suitable conditions, the Spitfire XII could indeed deal with low-level raiders.

On 21 May 1943, No. 41 Squadron moved to Biggin Hill, staying one week before moving to the advanced airfield at Friston, near which most Fw 190 raids were taking place. Friston had grass runways and was far from suitable for the Spitfire XIIs, but stand-bys with the pilots at cockpit readiness began on 29 May. Not until 4 June did action come.

At 11.25 hours some eighteen Fw 190s came out of the sun at low level. This time the raiders had been observed soon enough, allowing eight Spitfires of 41 Squadron to scramble in time to intercept. They waded into the enemy force, splitting it and preventing some raiders from bombing Eastbourne. Anti-aircraft guns also opened up over the town and claimed three Fw 190s while at sea Flg. Off. J. Solack, a Pole, destroyed another. A further Fw 190 was damaged by Flg. Off. D. H. Smith.

Such was the frequency of enemy forays that No. 91 Squadron was now flying standing patrols and was called upon for some scrambles. On 31 May alone, forty-seven sorties, totalling forty hours of flying, were made, and because of this, squadron excitement mounted early on the morning of 2 June. Shortly after 05.15 hours reports came through that an Fw 190 force had headed across the Thames Estuary out to sea and was heading for landfall on the Suffolk coast. Before they could be intercepted the eighteen Fw 190s bombed and strafed Ipswich, Felixstowe and Holland-on-Sea from 0 feet, and also dropped bombs in the sea off Orfordness. Royal Air Force fighters were too late getting away to stop the raid. Six Typhoons of 609 Squadron came within sight of the enemy only when the enemy was nearing Ostend and about to come under a welcoming umbrella of eighteen Fw 190s.

At Hawkinge it had been thought that 91 Squadron might be able to fly fast enough to cut off the enemy's retreat and four Spitfires took off but were too late to aid the Typhoons. Instead, they patrolled the Hastings–Dungeness area in case of a diversionary raid.

Just before 11.25 hours on 4 June it was the turn of 41 Squadron to engage a fighter-bomber raid. Eighteen Fw 190s raced over Eastbourne bombing and strafing the town. No. 41 Squadron's swift response enabled them to intercept the raiders just as they were developing their attack; some had to jettison their bombs and flee fast. In addition to No. 41 Squadron's four Sections, comprising eight aircraft, No. 91 Squadron had the same number of pilots flying but they were too far away to engage the raid. Defending guns at Eastbourne claimed three Fw 190s and another fell to Flg. Off. J. Solack of No. 41 Squadron who caught up with the quarry off Le Treport and shot it into the sea. Another was badly crippled by Flg. Off. D. H. Smith.

Despite losses, the enemy evidently considered that his attacks were worth continuing for they were tying down R.A.F. fighters and generally causing annoyance. At 13.30 hours on 6 June another Fw 190 intrusion was directed at

Eastbourne. This time it seemed that most of the Fw 190s were giving withdrawal cover to the fighter-bomber force. No. 41 Squadron scrambled four Spitfires but had no success. No. 91 Squadron had, a short time earlier, sent two Sections to patrol the Hastings area where Flg. Off. R. Johnson had to force land due to engine trouble. Moments later an Fw 190 was spotted near Eastbourne. Plt. Off. D. H. Davy and Sgt. Watterson gave chase, and reached the Le Treport area before they were able to catch and destroy the enemy. To thwart further activity, standing patrols were flown in thundery conditions until dusk.

There was now a lull in the activity of the fighter-bombers for they were training for night operations against Britain. Both Spitfire XII squadrons continued defensive patrols and 'Jim Crow' sorties until 16 June when a Typhoon pilot of No. 3 Squadron was believed to have come down in the sea 15–20 miles south-east of Dover. Flg. Off. G. Stenborg, R.N.Z.A.F., and Sgt. Fraser, both of 91 Squadron, left Hawkinge on a sea search and soon located him. They radioed their position and at 06.10 hours a Walrus of 277 Squadron took off from Hawkinge with an escort of four more Spitfires of 91 Squadron to try to rescue the pilot. A safe landing was made by the Walrus and he was picked up, but the swell was so heavy that the Walrus was unable to take off and therefore began to taxi back to Dover. However, soon after the journey began, trouble developed fast. About twenty aircraft were spotted some way off to the south. They were Fw 190s flying at about 2,000 feet, no warning of which had been received by No. 91 Squadron. Yellow Section quickly turned and raced into the enemy formation. A fine mêlée developed. Flg. Off. R. Nash quickly claimed two Fw 190s by which time Flg. Off. V. P. Seydel, a Belgian, had been shot down. On re-forming it was found that Sgt. Mitchell was missing too. Radar traces of the battle showed that four aircraft in all had gone into the sea and after consideration of the claims and losses it was agreed that Flg. Off. R. Nash had destroyed and damaged an Fw 190 and that another engaged by Seydel had come down off Wissant.

White Section of No. 91 Squadron had reached the scene too late for battle. At 07.10 hours Stenborg and Fraser were ordered off to search for Seydel, and for Nash who had been seen to bale out. Red Section found Nash and by repeatedly diving towards him attracted the attention of high-speed launch HSL 2547 to the spot. He was picked up, his injuries including a broken arm and leg and back wounds. He was safely taken to Dover hospital. The Walrus, too, made a safe return with its passenger.

The following days were, for both squadrons, packed with patrols, alarms and 'Jim Crows' without engagements ensuing. The absence of the Fw 190s resulted in new employment for the Spitfire XII squadrons. They would form a Wing under Tangmere control and fly bomber-support missions at medium levels. No. 41 Squadron moved into West Hampnett on 21 June and No. 91 Squadron was installed there a week later.

With the daylight bombing campaign increasing in intensity and operations becoming more complex, their sheer numbers began to make great demands upon Fighter Command, which was now providing aircraft for home defence,

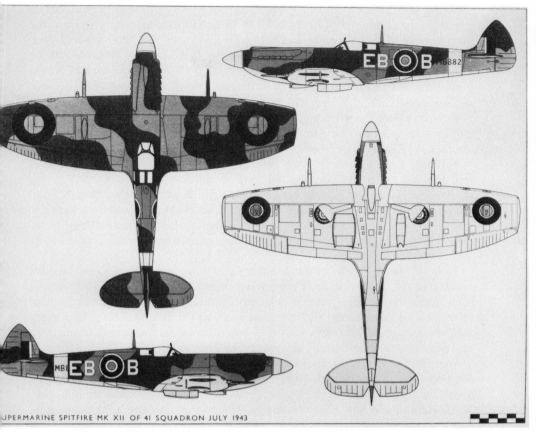

SUPERMARINE SPITFIRE MK XII OF 41 SQUADRON JULY 1943

3. Supermarine Spitfire Mk. XII of 41 Squadron, July 1943. The upper surfaces are Dark Green (dark tint) and Ocean Grey, with the under surfaces Medium Sea Grey. Squadron identity letters, the spinner and the band encircling the rear fuselage, are a very pale shade of Sky

sweeps, strafing of ground targets, support for day raids by 2 Group and was also having to meet increasing requests to give fighter cover to the Americans during the day raids over the Continent. So far these operations had mainly been by Fortresses and Liberators to which the R.A.F. had given much fighter cover and some escort. American fighters were still few in number and as short of range as those of the R.A.F.—not to mention less experienced. The Fortresses and Liberators, though, flew at higher levels than those at which the Spitfire XIIs could best give close escort, and at lower levels the day bombers had to rely upon Spitfire Vs for protection.

The new B-26 Marauders arrived on the scene at this time and so, to give some boost to the fighter-escort squadrons, it was decided to use the Mk. XII squadrons to give medium-level support to bombers of 2 Group and some support to their escorting fighters. This released some Spitfire IXs—now in service in worthwhile numbers—to give top cover, where their performance was good. On the evening of 26 June 1943, No. 41 Squadron commenced flying in the new role, lending support to the withdrawal of sixty B-17s which had been bombing Le Mans. The squadron, led by Wg. Cdr. R. Thomas, Wing Commander Flying at Tangmere, with Sqn. Ldr. T. F. Neil at the head of No. 41 Squadron, flew behind the returning Fortresses to mop up any enemy fighters but none materialized.

Two days later, No. 91 Squadron arrived at West Hampnett and the following day both squadrons flew for the first time as a Wing, giving rear support to another B-17 raid on Le Mans. Again, enemy fighters were absent.

Typhoon fighter-bombers were currently being used to attack enemy fighter airfields and on 1 July the two Mk. XII squadrons found themselves giving medium-level support over the target when eight 'Bomphoons' of Nos. 175 and 181 Squadrons shot up and bombed Abbeville, while Courtrai and Poix were also raided. Fighter sweeps in support of day bomber operations, more 'Bomphoon' cover and rear support to returning B-17s interspersed with air/sea rescue sorties all followed.

Ramrod 144 was flown on the evening of 16 July, and proved to be the most eventful so far. The Spitfire XII Wing was detailed to fly the Third Fighter Sweep, such operations taking place in wide arcs ahead of and around the bomber formation and its escorts. The intention was that the Spitfire XIIs would sweep the Poix area at 10,000 feet while the bombers crossed the Channel, in the hope that the Spitfires would catch any enemy fighters taking off.

The Spitfire XII Wing crossed in over Le Treport as planned and when it reached Poix some Fw 190s were seen taking off. Red 3 and 4, Flg. Off. G. Stenborg and Flg. Off. J. A. Anstie, dived after them, followed by Wg. Cdr. R. H. Harries and Sgt. J. T. Watterson. The first two, unable to make contact with the foe, climbed away. Harries and his companion then saw two other Fw 190s climbing after take off but as they positioned to fire at one it abruptly banked and crashed, bursting into flames. Both pilots then made a battle climb to rejoin the formation whose sweep then proceeded. Each time the Spitfire formation broke for more combat the enemy evaded battle.

On days when the weather was cloudy and rainy small numbers of Spitfire XIIs flew low-level strafing flights to France, shooting at targets of opportunity during such *Rhubarbs*. Stenborg and Fraser flew such sorties on 17 July and found a train near Morseline. They attacked the engine and its box trucks four times, leaving the engine a mass of steam. Next day it was fine and *Ramrod* operations were ordered. In the early evening, while 'Bomphoons' of 83 Group attacked Abbeville the Tangmere Wing swept Poix–Abbeville above them. They again crossed in over Le Treport at 9,000 feet and, five miles inland, spotted 'Bomphoons' heading into flak. Turning towards Poix the Spitfire pilots saw about twenty-five enemy aircraft coming up to attack. They were mainly Bf 109s which climbed rapidly, swung around and dived, firing on No. 41 Squadron, and then hurtled past No. 91 Squadron who were flying lower.

Flg. Off. T. Slack and Flg. Off. R. Hogarth of No. 41 Squadron had both been shot down when the enemy bounced their squadron, and Fisher's aircraft was riddled. Wing Commander Harries saw three Bf 109s above to port and led his Section to the attack. He, with Watterson and Round, fired at one inconclusively, then Harries shot the tail off a second Bf 109. The third enemy fighter half rolled and dived away with Blue 1 on his tail. Harries closed to 200 yards firing, getting hits in the wings before it dived away blazing. Meanwhile Wg. Cdr. Thomas had climbed to engage, taking the rest of Yellow Section and two of Red Section with him after twelve Bf 109s circling above the Spitfires. A Bf 109 dived fast by the circling force and Yellow 3 went after him but staked no claim. By the time the Spitfire XIIs had reached the enemy's height the latter had left the scene. Four of them chased Wg. Cdr. Harries who had reached the coast by the time he had shaken off his pursuers. Just before reaching Beachy Head he came alongside a Typhoon which suddenly turned on to its back. The pilot baled out and was luckily picked up by HSL 145. Harries was credited with two Bf 109s shot down and one damaged. Following this operation the Mk. XII Wing flew in seven more *Ramrods* before July ended uneventfully. Such operations interspersed with a few *Rodeos* and *Rhubarbs* continued until 24 August before any more claims were lodged.

Both squadrons took off from West Hampnett on a bomber escort to Bernay on the evening of 24 August. They climbed to 9,000 feet at the French coast and flew in level at 240 m.p.h. I.A.S., entering France over Caborg and flying via Bernay to Beaumont. There they orbited and two Fw 190s dived on to the rear of No. 91 Squadron. Stenborg and Flt. Sgt. Mulcany of the squadron abruptly turned to engage the attackers, causing the leading pilot to bale out. Meanwhile an attack had developed on two more of 91's aircraft so the others turned to engage the enemy. No. 41 Squadron maintained top cover preventing another formation of Fw 190s some height above from attacking. The Fw 190 which was destroyed brought the total of claims by Tangmere squadrons since the start of the war to 700 enemy aircraft, almost certainly an inflated total.

The largest 'spoof' of the war was about to commence and its purpose was threefold. Firstly a very intensive operational campaign waged against a variety of targets in France would surely bring the enemy fighters to battle. Secondly, and as the highlight of the operation, a large fleet of landing-craft and ships would be assembled in the Channel to make a feint of landing on the Pas de Calais as if to open the 'second front'. Thirdly, in this situation the enemy would surely react and reveal tactics which he had laid down for such an eventuality.

The whole operation, code-named *Starkey*, would give experience to the Allies for when they were to invade France. *Starkey* commenced on 25 August, the role of the Spitfire XIIs changing little as *Ramrods* continued but at a faster rate. On 27 August Wg. Cdr. R. H. Harries led the two squadrons in a new role, protecting bombers against frontal attack. Nothing was seen of the enemy, but two Spitfires were lost due to technical malfunctions. The first four days of September found the Mk. XIIs at Lympne, flying patrols to protect shipping and Bostons laying smoke over the 'landing force'.

For most of the fighter force *Starkey* was a bitter disappointment since the enemy did not react much, possibly suspecting that it was a fraud. As regards combat, the Tangmere squadrons were more involved than most. Their first engagement came on 2 September. The Wing carried out an evening escort to bombers raiding Hesdin. On the way to the target Flt. Lt. I. G. Matthew and Flt. Lt. G. W. Bond turned back, the former's engine giving trouble. Four miles from Le Touquet four Bf 109s, their pilots probably thinking the Spitfires easy game, attacked them—one coming head on and the other astern on to Matthew who opened fire at the first attacker, sending it rolling over. It crashed on the French shore. The other two now attacked Bond from astern. He shook them off only to see Matthew being attacked. In a favourable position, he shot the enemy off the tail of Matthew and the German fighter crashed into the sea. Then the Spitfires raced for home.

Period A of *Starkey* had consisted of attacks on airfields. Period B commenced on 4 September 1943 with marshalling-yards as targets. At 17.50 hours on this day the Spitfire XII Wing left to provide escort cover to thirty-six B-26s attacking St. Pol. After some good bombing the 'beehive' left for home. Near Le Touquet the close escort was set upon by some twenty Fw 190s. The two Spitfire XII squadrons dived to join the dogfights, as a result of which the Tangmere and Merston Wings between them were credited with nine enemy fighters shot down and three damaged. Birbeck and his No. 4, Sgt. P. Graham, orbited the battle scene then picked out an Fw 190 at 5,000 feet. Birbeck gave chase, the enemy climbed away in a turn and Birbeck closed opening fire. The Fw 190 rolled and the chase was on, at 355 m.p.h. I.A.S. As Birbeck closed to 300 yards he continued firing whereupon the Fw 190 flew into some trees, cartwheeled and smashed itself. Another Fw 190 had meanwhile drawn alongside him and turned to fire, but with all his ammunition used he turned for his base. Graham left his No. 3 to follow a second Fw 190 over Étaples airfield but was hit in the rudder by light flak and had to bring his Spitfire to a forced landing at Ford. Flt. Lt. A. A. Glen was seen to bale out and the A.S.R. service soon fished him out of the water. Birbeck's Fw 190 brought No. 41 Squadron's credited score to 150 in total.

When Kynaston and Sell of No. 91 Squadron had dived to take part in the fight, two Fw 190s latched on to their tails. They were shaken off, whereupon one of the enemy turned his attention to another Spitfire which abruptly turned to fire upon his adversary from 200 yards. It burst into flames and its pilot baled out.

Stenborg followed two Fw 190s into a steep dive from which they roared fast skywards. He scored hits on the tail of one fighter, then directed fire at the other. Firing from fifty yards now, he saw plentiful hits before the Fw 190 went into the sea. No. 91 Squadron suffered no loss, but Plt. Off. R. McPhee had to land at Friston with technical trouble. The total score in this engagement was four Fw 190s shot down and one damaged by 402 Squadron, a Bf 109 and an Fw 190 claimed by 416 Squadron and a Bf 109 damaged by Wg. Cdr. Chadburn in addition to those which fell to the Spitfire XIIs.

High cover was being given to a Mitchell *Ramrod* early on 8 September to Vitry-en-Artois, a target needing relatively deep penetration. Stenborg had

8.   Spitfire XII MB882 seen here at a later date than in the previous picture, and wearing the markings of 41 Squadron. 'EB:D' MB858 served with 41 Squadron from September 1943 until late in 1944

oxygen trouble near Lille and he descended to 3,000 feet where he and his Section were sitting-targets for four Fw 190s which jumped them, shooting down Plt. Off. C. R. Fraser. Flg. Off. D. H. Smith then had to retire from the scene since his radio was giving trouble. This left Blumer and Stenborg to fight it out. Blumer attacked two Fw 190s; one was seen going down with smoke pouring from its cowling, and Stenborg saw it crash.

The intensive operations of the previous fortnight culminated in the large amphibious exercise in the Channel mounted from the early hours of 9 September. There were three main areas of operations: Boulogne and Le Touquet (where attacks were made upon the beaches by medium bombers), the assault convoy which had left Dungeness (including landing-craft which had set out from many south-coast ports), and three convoys of large vessels in the Spithead–Beachy Head areas.

The Spitfire XII Wing came to readiness at 05.15 hours with the squadrons on top line beneath a sky already teeming with aircraft. Tangmere's Typhoons were escorting the assault convoy while Mustangs were guarding the large ships. Spitfire VIIs went after two Huns who were looking at the scene from a great height, and then it was the Spitfire XII Wing's turn to mount the third patrol over the assault convoy. Ten miles off Conches the armada turned back behind a smoke screen. There had been no enemy response, and *Starkey* soon closed uneventfully.

The next engagements for the Spitfire XII squadrons came on 16 September when *Ramrod 223* was mounted against Beaumont-le-Roger. All was uneventful until near the target when German fighters appeared. Kynaston led No. 41 Squadron to engage and then an Fw 190 was chased at tree-top level before it crashed. On the way home Sgt. Mulcany had engine trouble and Blumer closed to cover him. Six Fw 190s swept in to pick them off, but Blumer drew away fast and soon shot one down. Mulcany, however, was without good fortune and was shot down twelve miles west of Le Hay. It was too late for the A.S.R. service to locate him. Blue Section of No. 91 Squadron had broken away to help out and Flg. Off. B. B. Newman claimed one enemy fighter, but the battle was too fast for No. 91 Squadron to arrive in strength and in time.

The next fight took place on 19 September. It was cloudy above the bomber force and, virtually cut off, the Spitfire XIIs had to deal with nearly fifty enemy fighters. No. 91 Squadron managed to drive them off only to face another thirty. Dogfights developed over Lille. Wg. Cdr. Harries destroyed an Fw 190 and Flt. Lt. J. C. Doll damaged another before being shot down when climbing away. Flg. Off. G. W. Bond was also shot down and could not be rescued, but Blumer who had to bale out off Deal was picked up by a launch. No. 41 Squadron lost Flt. Sgt. May, last seen heading into battle.

On 22 September the Spitfire XII Wing again gave fighter cover during a *Ramrod.* After the bombing the enemy fighters were seen below the Tangmere Wing, who dived upon them, Harries quickly making a claim. A second enemy aircraft was soon spinning away. No. 41 Squadron joined the formation as it headed back to the bombers and found that an attack on them was about to develop. Birbeck and Sgt. Vann chased three Fw 190s but although Vann saw some hits on his target he was unable to catch it. Flg. Off. D. H. Smith fired at an Fw 190 and saw strikes, then one of the enemy's cannon blew up and the Fw 190 went down. Newman closed upon another and Sqn. Ldr. N. A. Kynaston reported that it had crashed. Meanwhile Birbeck was in trouble and, having been hit over Quillerboeuf, began to think that he would never reach home. He turned out to sea, considering this his best hope, and the enemy following him gave up the chase. Birbeck came out over Trouville and twenty miles south of Ford had to bale out. Two Typhoon pilots witnessed the event—and the big splash when his sixteen and a half stone landed in the water. He reached his dinghy, but as he began to bail out the water he fell into the sea again. He clambered aboard once more and, since his position was known, he was rescued by a launch after two hours at sea.

Next day it was No. 91 Squadron's turn to engage in battle while No. 41 Squadron maintained close escort to a formation of bombers. Again, action followed the bombing. Sqn. Ldr. Kynaston found himself in a dogfight, with his No. 2 aiding him, and claimed an Fw 190. Flt. Lt. Doll claimed another and a third fell to Stenborg, a Bf 109.

The first *Ramrod* on 24 September also proved eventful for both Spitfire XII squadrons. Beauvais was the bombers' target and dogfights ensued during the entire return journey. Flt. Lt. R. S. Easby and Flg. Off. A. G. O'Shaughnessy dived after two fighters but, unable to overtake, hared after another Bf 109 which

9.   After service with 41 Squadron MB853 served with the Air Fighting Development
Unit from October 1944 to August 1945, in whose hands it is seen here although it
retains squadron letters

O'Shaughnessy soon despatched in flames. Flying low, they now had another
Bf 109 cross their path. Easby took it with a quarter attack and it disintegrated.

A second *Ramrod* on the same day, during which seventy-two B-26s bombed
Beauvais, was equally eventful. The Spitfire XII squadrons were providing escort
cover, but this was costly for No. 91 Squadron. Forty enemy fighters were seen
near the target. About fifteen dived out of the sun past the Wing then another
twenty or so tried to bounce it. Kynaston, Dorrell and Maridor each claimed an
Fw 190, Kynaston's broke up after a three-second burst; Maridor's crashed in a
wood. An audacious head-on attack put Stenborg's Spitfire out of action and
seconds later others of the squadron saw it curling away streaming glycol.

Wg. Cdr. Harries was leading the Wing on this occasion and, when the first ten
fighters dived past the escort after the B-26s, Flt. Lt. A. A. Glen led No. 41
Squadron after them, forcing them to veer away to the right and away from the
Marauders. A mixture of Spitfire Vs, IXs and XIIs then closed into a major
dogfight, as a result of which No. 41 Squadron claimed two Fw 190s plus a
probable and another damaged. Glen had deputized for Harries whose radio was
troublesome. He soon crippled an Fw 190 which then exploded, careering into
another, both of which then disintegrated in a gigantic flash. Flg. Off. H. R.
Parry, though, was missing. Apart from an inconclusive engagement on 27
September this was the last battle during that month.

When the scores for September 1943 were totted up it was found that No. 91 Squadron was top scorer in Fighter Command, and that Tangmere was the top-scoring Sector. It was to that parent station that both squadrons moved in the first week of October.

This came at a time when it had been decided to use Spitfires as fighter-bombers against tactical targets in France. Being a low-altitude fighter the Spitfire XII seemed ideally suited to the new task. Accordingly, MB878 had been delivered to Boscombe Down early in September 1943 for trials to assess its performance when carrying a 500 lb. bomb on its centre line. This Spitfire had a Griffon IV engine whose limitations were: maximum power for all-out level flight at 2,750 revs. with +12 lb./sq. in. boost, and maximum for M.S. cruise in weak mixture 2,400 revs. with +6 lb./sq. in. boost. The 10 ft. 5 in. four-bladed propeller with left hand rotation was a Rotol Hydraulic V.P. R13/4F5/6. At take off for trials the weight of the aircraft was 7,270 lb. without the rack and bomb, 7,772 lb. with both fitted. Without the external load the c.g. was now 5·8 in. aft, 6·2 in. aft with rack and bomb in place.

At 14,000 ft. the all-out level speed of this aircraft with neither rack nor bomb was 372 m.p.h. T.A.S. Its maximum speed in F.S. gear was 391 m.p.h. T.A.S. at 19,000 ft., falling away to 382 m.p.h. T.A.S. at 22,000 ft. With the rack in place these figures were reduced to 361 m.p.h. T.A.S. at 14,000 ft. and peaked at 19,000 ft. to 380 m.p.h. T.A.S. With the bomb being carried maximum speed reached was 371 m.p.h. T.A.S. at 17,900 ft. The best cruise performance without the rack and in M.S. gear was 341 m.p.h. T.A.S. at 9,000 ft., and 333 m.p.h. T.A.S. at the same height with the bomb being carried. Trials continued until December 1943. Although the aircraft was cleared for fighter-bomber employment no operational use was made of this role.

Meanwhile there had been no respite for the two operational squadrons. At the start of October 1943 the weather was poor and *Rhubarbs* took place. On 3 October it improved sufficiently to permit participation in four *Ramrods*, making it the busiest day ever for the Spitfire XII Wing, yet profitless as regards combat. No engagements took place until 20 October when what began as an uneventful day turned out to be the best ever for the Spitfire XII Wing.

Rodeo 263 commenced at 09.10 hours when both squadrons left on a fighter sweep in the Tricqueville–Bernay–Beaumont area with Gp. Cpt. Grisham leading and Wg. Cdr. Harries as his No. 2. They encountered accurate flak at the enemy coast which forced Birbeck to turn about, owing to flak damage, and Graham escorted him home. The formation crossed in over Cap d'Antifer, climbed to 18,000 ft. over Bernay and swept down towards Evreux. Between Rouen and Evreux, twenty-five to thirty Bf 109Gs and Fw 190s dived from about 13,000 feet and out of the sun. The Spitfires turned to port, climbing, with the enemy aircraft opening fire at extreme range. Then the enemy aircraft dived steeply and the Spitfires gave chase, fierce fighting ensuing. Harries had soon bagged two Bf 109s and Flg. Off. B. Newman and Flg. Off. R. Collis each claimed another. Flg. Off. P. Cowell shot down an Fw 190 from which the pilot baled out. No. 91 Squadron's share of success amounted to Sqn. Ldr. Kynaston and Flg. Off. J. C. S. Doll each getting an Fw 190 while Flg. Off. R. S. Nash and Flt. Sgt. R. Blumer each destroyed a Bf 109G. In a matter of moments the entire Wing was disorganized and after the engagement the Spitfires made their own ways back to base with a claim of nine enemy aircraft without loss to themselves. Battle scores like that of 20 October 1943 were rare over France, and never again did the Mk. XIIs acquire such a tally. Indeed, that day's fighting was the last time that the Spitfire XII Wing engaged in such action.

One of the reasons for this was that the enemy was now fast building his V-1 sites, attacks upon which attracted tremendous Allied response so that *Rodeos* became fewer. Also, fighter defence of these sites was impracticable. Instead, the enemy brought along a large number of anti-aircraft guns of mixed calibres and ranges, for they knew that it was more important to prevent the Allies knocking out the sites than to shoot down a few fighters and bombers at loss to themselves. Additionally, the Germans needed fighters more and more for home defence.

Thus, to the end of 1943, the Spitfire XII Wing found itself escorting 2 Group and the U.S. 9th A.A.F. during its *Noball* campaign, and sometimes providing cover to escorting Spitfire Vs. Thirty-two operations in support of *Ramrods* were flown before 1943 ended with an uneventful sweep. Usually the two squadrons provided escort to bombers or their fighter protection. Occasionally they made wide sweeps to fend off possible attacks from bases further to the south, east or west of the area under attack, as many as six such sweeps being arranged to cover one *Ramrod* operation. At no time during November or December 1943 did the Luftwaffe rise to battle.

The effectiveness of low-level strikes on the V-weapon sites by Mosquito VI fighter-bombers become evident by the end of 1943, and from January 1944 the six squadrons of 2 T.A.F. struck at such targets in northern France. The Mosquito squadrons concentrated on low-level operations, but, although the Mosquitoes were fast at this level, there was always the risk that enemy fighters might sweep down upon them and thus pick them off. It made sense to give them an escort—and what better than to utilize the Spitfire XIIs? Operations for them then took place throughout January 1944 interspersed with medium-level *Ramrod* support. During a fighter sweep on 21 January eight Fw 190s were seen, but no fighting took place.

Unlike almost all the other Spitfire squadrons, Nos. 41 and 91 had never left the front line during 1943 for any rest period of practice fighting, or to reside in quieter parts of the country. Such a break, however, came in February 1944, and on the afternoon of 6 February, after a patrol over Mosquitoes, No. 41 Squadron left for the Armament Practice Camp at Southend, and No. 91 Squadron retired for rest at Hutton Cranswick in Lincolnshire.

This was virtually the end of the Spitfire XII Wing, for although the two squadrons returned to Tangmere—and between 21 and 28 February flew five more bomber escorts—the days of the Wing were already numbered.

There were two reasons for this. One was the imminent introduction of the second type of Griffon-engined Spitfire, the Mk. XIV, to No. 91 Squadron. The other was the problem of providing spares for the remaining Mk. XIIs. They had given excellent service, were not equalled by any other Spitfire variant in the low-level role, and might still be useful against low-level intruders attempting to interfere with 2 T.A.F. daylight activities. This last seemed possible because of the Luftwaffe night attacks in what became known as the Baby Blitz. So, while No. 91 Squadron withdrew from the fight to re-equip with Mk. XIVs, No. 41 Squadron soldiered on with XIIs at Tangmere with a fresh pool of aircraft to draw upon.

Between March and June 1944, No. 41 Squadron took part in a number of *Ramrods*, its aircraft mixing with Mk. IXs at medium levels where there was a basic difference in performance to overcome. They also flew Typhoon escorts and participated in *Rhubarbs*.

From 1 March there was a reduced state of readiness, No. 41 Squadron keeping one Section at fifteen-minute alert to intercept intruders. On the morning of 11 March the squadron cleared its dispersals at Tangmere, now full of Typhoons, and, forming the Cross of St. Omer, flew across their home of such long standing and moved to Friston to resume readiness.

The weather of 13 March was bad, with as strong a gale as might ever be expected in the area. The squadron requested that it might not be scrambled except in extreme emergency for it was dangerous to fly. Suddenly an order to scramble came at 11.30 hours, but before Flg. Off. Wain had taxied ten yards his aircraft was blown on to its back. Later Flg. Off. D. J. Shea was lucky to get off. Flg. Off. R. P. Harding and Flg. Off. H. Cook followed him. Harding was soon re-called leaving the other two to make an urgently required air/sea rescue search. Return entailed a night landing at Friston which was a difficult procedure. Somehow Cook made it, but as Shea came swaying in his engine cut. He stalled and was killed when the Spitfire plunged into the ground.

Three days later six pilots of 'A' Flight were ordered to escort a Sea Otter of No. 277 Squadron flying an A.S.R. sortie over the Somme Estuary, where a Canadian pilot of No. 401 Squadron was known to have come down. Under fire from shore batteries the Sea Otter landed in the river estuary, and picked up the Canadian while the Spitfires orbited. Another A.S.R. support operation was also flown on 16 March. This time the squadron was ordered to protect a Walrus which had picked up ten Americans from a crashed B-17 which had come down in the sea off Dieppe. With such a heavy load take off was impossible and a Sea Otter was sent to assist, taking aboard half the crew. Covered by No. 41 Squadron's Spitfires the amphibians managed to get airborne and were safely escorted home.

A number of enemy reconnaissance aircraft operated over the south coast in April, but No. 41 Squadron was never fast enough to engage them. After some *Ramrods* No. 41 Squadron moved to Bolt Head on 29 April 1944 to patrol defensively over Portland and support and cover operations by naval Seafires.

Rhubarbs were being carried out with mixed results. On 31 May Blue Section, led by Flt. Lt. Slack who had made a safe return to his squadron after being shot down, set off for the airfields at Vannes, Gael and Kerlin Bastard where Ju 188s were said to be based. No enemy bombers were found, but at Kerlin Bastard flak was heavy enough to split the formation open. Lorries, trains and a 500-ton ship were attacked.

The main preoccupation in the days immediately preceding the Normandy landings concerned stand-bys for possible action against Allied shipping, and reconnaissances to watch enemy shipping movements around Guernsey. On 2 June Flg. Off. Wagner and Flt. Sgt. Stevenson left on a shipping reconnaissance to St. Peter Port and St. Malo. They flew to Brehan Island, meeting flak from its round tower. Wagner's radiator was hit so he pulled up and headed for home. North of Herm he was forced to bale out. Stevenson alerted base and orbited his companion until A.S.R. Spitfires arrived. Later, Yellow Section of No. 41 Squadron arrived overhead to give Wagner cover. A Warwick was then vectored to the scene and dropped a lifeboat. Its parachutes failed to collapse and the lifeboat drifted out of Wagner's reach. Later that day four Spitfire XIIs covered the arrival of a Walrus which alighted and rescued Wagner.

For many squadrons D-Day was their busiest for months, but for No. 41 Squadron it was uneventful. Pairs of Spitfires continued shipping protection patrols from mid-morning and escorted a Warwick A.S.R. aircraft on patrol.

The following day Red and Blue Sections took off at 08.40 hours to escort 'Bomphoons' of 263 Squadron sent to attack the quays at St. Peter Port, Guernsey. Three of the four Spitfires received hits from flak and Flg. Off. Robinson was forced to bale out when his Spitfire was hit in the radiator. Flt. Lt. Collis orbited and managed to drop his dinghy to Robinson who had lost his when baling out. Warwicks came on to the scene and dropped two lifeboats, but both drifted away downwind. Robinson was seen to fall from his dinghy, but soon clambered aboard again. It took a Walrus eighteen attempts before it could land, by which time Robinson had tragically died.

Patrols and *Rhubarbs* continued into June. On 12 June Flt. Lt. Thiele led Green Section on a *Rhubarb* to St. Brieuc. Flg. Off. Payn and Flg. Off. Balasse attacked and damaged a two-gun armoured car near St. Gille; other ground targets were then attacked, and Balasse blew up a locomotive. About ten miles south of base he baled out and was picked up a few minutes later by a Walrus. On 18 June an early shipping reconnaissance was flown off Lisadrier and Abverlasche; Flt. Lt. Slack's engine cut and he had to bale out. Blue 2 circled then returned to base to refuel. After searching for his colleague Flt. Sgt. Ware once more ran out of fuel and baled out too. Slack was soon rescued by a Walrus and the same aircraft picked up Ware. It was too rough for the Walrus to take off and both pilots had to be brought ashore by a launch.

In the early hours of 15 June 1944 the first V-1 flying bombs were despatched against London. Just how to deal with them provoked urgent, intense discussion. Full details of their performance and mode of employment had yet to come to hand. They were fast and came in very low. What better, then, than to pit the Spitfire XIIs, excellent low performers, against them? Accordingly on 19 June Sqn. Ldr. R. H. Chapman, who had taken command of No. 41 Squadron on 28 May, led his squadron to West Malling, situated in line with the V-1 tracks to the capital.

The main question was whether the Spitfire XII was fast enough to catch the V-1s. The answer was—barely so. If the pilot took up good station higher he could dive on his quarry and an effective interception would be achieved, as Wg. Cdr. R. H. Chapman recalled: 'We were the slowest of the aircraft on the job—the Tempests and Typhoons had the legs of us by about fifteen to twenty knots, and so we tried all ways to get a few extra knots. We took the rear view mirror off and had the aircraft polished like a car, but it made no difference. So we thought that if we lightened the aircraft that might help. We took out all the armour plating and reduced the amount of ammunition that we carried, but not one extra knot of speed did we get. That we were mystified and puzzled is to say the least. Then a "boffin" came up with the answer. By removing the armour plate we had moved the c.g. and so altered the angle of attack and consequently increased the drag, so that one thing cancelled out the other. We gave up after that.

'The Spitfire XII—as far as I recall—had no really big vices. It was a bit nose heavy with the extra weight of the Griffon, and swung quite a lot on take off. Apart from that I remember it was a lovely aircraft for aerobatics, with the clipped wings and extra power. It had a rated altitude of about 15,000 feet, so, naturally, we were always used for low-level work.'

On 20 June a most intensive period of daylight operations against the flying-bombs began and thirteen patrols were flown by No. 41 Squadron. First success came to Plt. Off. N. P. Gibbs who, in the evening, saw a V-1 twelve miles south of Beachy Head. It was seven miles ahead at 3,000 feet and he closed to 200 yards, gave it a burst, and saw it explode by the Eastbourne Road at Friston. Later that evening Flg. Off. K. R. Curtis shot off the port wing of a V-1, the flying-bomb coming down near Battle. Gibbs claimed his second V-1 next day when nineteen patrols were flown. On 22 June Flt. Sgt. C. Robertson shot down his first V-1, six miles north of Pevensey, and Flt. Lt. C. R. Birbeck and Flt. Lt. Anderson destroyed one between them north of Maidstone at 18.25 hours.

Success rates were not particularly high, for the weapons came fast and low, were difficult to detect, required utmost vigilance to intercept and were very hard to catch—and they needed to be destroyed in open country, which brought severe limitations. Flt. Lt. T. Spencer shot down a V-1 north of Hastings at dusk on 23 June, Gibbs destroyed his third at 06.15 hours on 24 June south of Hastings and at dusk that day Flt. Sgt. R. L. Short, after being ordered to base, saw the tell-tale flames from the flying-bomb behind him. He pulled up, then gave a burst and his strike brought him success. (Wg. Cdr. Chapman recalled how a scientist came up with the idea of wearing tinted goggles, amber in tone, the theory being that the contrast would show up the colour of the flames more vividly—but the idea did not prove successful.) Flt. Lt. T. Spencer destroyed his second V-1 during the same patrol. Next day twenty-five patrols were flown. To 6 July No. 41 Squadron had been credited with thirteen and a half V-1s destroyed, which put them in twelfth place in the scoring league table which was headed by No. 3 Squadron who claimed $163\frac{1}{2}$. But the Griffon Spitfires, Mks. XII and XIV, had, between them, been credited with a score of $161\frac{1}{2}$.

On some days the weather was too bad for any patrols, but still the bombs

10.   The clipped wing of the Mk.XII is clearly visible here as MB882 banks away

came. When Portsmouth and Southampton began to come under fire, No. 41 Squadron moved back to West Hampnett and Friston, and successes came at a steady rate. On 8 July, for instance, the score was opened at dawn. Flt. Sgt. P. W. Chatting shot one down in the Thames Estuary. It exploded, holing his aircraft in the radiator, wing and propeller. In the evening Gibbs destroyed his fourth V-1. Flg. Off. R. E. Anderson and Flg. Off. A. S. Appleton shared the squadron's twenty-first success on 9 July.

Two days later No. 41 Squadron returned to the area of the main line of fire when it arrived at Lympne. As Wg. Cdr. Chapman recalled: 'At this point in time the A.A. guns were still deployed in a belt round the coast which made life rather embarrassing if one got on to a V-1 out to sea and started chasing it inland. The usual inter-Service argument ensued as to who was the more effective. However, the fighters won and the A.A. guns were moved back to the barrage balloons.'

On the day after the move to Lympne Sgt. P. W. Chatting scored his second success. Despite a period of poor weather, successes continued. In the afternoon of 23 July Flg. Off. P. B. Graham and W. Off. A. S. Appleton were sent on patrol to relieve Payn and Balasse who had so far scored only one success. Barely were they on the patrol line when they were vectored on to a V-1 which Appleton shot down eight miles south of Bexhill.

The weather improved on 26 July. During the day the enemy appeared to be attempting to saturate the defences by firing salvoes of ten to twenty bombs at a time with intervals of one to two hours between each phase. Good weather meant that the fighters could cope. By day eighty V-1s were brought down overland to fighter fire and, in all 25 per cent of those launched within twenty-four hours were claimed. During this day No. 41 Squadron flew twenty-two patrols and in the evening Balasse made a kill bringing his score to four, to equal the squadron's other top scorer, Gibbs. Low cloud, though, made interception difficult at times. In the early evening of 29 July Balasse spotted a V-1 and dived upon it from 7,000 feet, narrowly missing it and coming up below the bomb. He suddenly looked up to see the weapon in a dive. It had been upset by his slipstream and was heading for the sea, the first to fall to No. 41 Squadron without a shot being fired. Later that evening Balasse was off again and after five minutes he latched on to another V-1 which he brought down one mile south-east of Woodchurch. This brought his total of kills to six, making him now 41's top scorer.

On 3 August, No. 41 Squadron's claims stood at thirty out of the $329\frac{1}{2}$ credited to Griffon Spitfires, out of the total credited to fighters, 1,578. Of these, $587\frac{1}{2}$ had fallen to Tempests, and $379\frac{1}{2}$ to Mosquitoes which operated at night. At this time the daylight hours were mainly cloudy and no clearances were setting in until late afternoon or evening. This made interception difficult or even impossible. The maximum firing effort by the enemy had come on 2–3 August when 286 V-1s were plotted in fourteen hours.

Flt. Sgt. I. T. Stevenson brought down a V-1 on 5 August north-west of Maidstone after firing at it and then tipping it over with his wing tip, not easy in a clipped-wing fighter. The flying-bomb patrols continued into August with a steady stream of claims. One of the most eventful interceptions befell Plt. Off. D. Graham early on 14 August. When on patrol he spotted a bomb 9,000 feet below. He dived and closed upon it but when he was about 250 yards away his Spitfire was suddenly thrown on to its back by slipstream from the V-1. After recovery he fired at the bomb, but aiming was difficult. He dived, firing as he pulled up without success. Then he decided to close and tip the weapon. Suddenly he saw the balloon belt ahead and had to relinquish the chase. However, the satisfaction of picking off a V-1 under the noses of a Meteor and two Tempests came to Graham on 16 August. Ten miles west-north-west of Tenterden he dived from 12,000 feet and saw his quarry being fired upon at extreme range but by other fighters. Zooming ahead of them he fired two short bursts and watched as the starboard wing of the bomb folded. The weapon came down near Wrotham, by which time Graham had to pull up fast to avoid the balloons.

The squadron offered a prize for the pilot who destroyed the fiftieth V-1. It was awarded to Flt. Lt. T. Spencer on 23 August. He took off at 08.05 hours and during his patrol destroyed the fiftieth and fifty-first V-1s to fall to No. 41 Squadron. The flying-bombs were coming in at 08.20 hours east of Folkestone, bursts of flak indicating their positions. Spencer closed, gave one a two-second burst and the V-1 then crashed on the railway line four miles south-east of Ashford. He then spotted another, four miles west of that town, dived from 10,000 feet and destroyed it near Harrietsham.

By now, No. 41 Squadron's fight against the flying-bombs was all but finished, the last success coming during the evening of 23 August to Flt. Lt. Lee, aided by a Tempest, ten miles north of Ashford. That same day No. 41 Squadron heard that it would be coming off V-1 patrols, and would resume the offensive role for which it would soon receive Spitfire XIVs.

When the final tally of claims was sorted, the squadron was credited with fifty-two flying-bombs, although in Fighter Command's opinion the total amounted to only thirty-nine and a half. In the light of full post-war investigation there came little to support either contention, but the squadron's claim appears to be the more likely of the two. Top scorers on No. 41 Squadron were Flt. Lt. T. Spencer and Flt. Lt. M. Balasse, the former with seven, the latter six. On 28 August, although No. 41 Squadron had been taken off *Diver* patrols, Spencer managed another kill to head the squadron's individual pilot total.

During the afternoon of 26 August the new phase of operations opened although No. 41 Squadron had managed a *Ranger* on 23 August. This new phase began with a low-level sweep to the Lille area, giving the pilots some practice along the lines on which they would operate Spitfire XIVs. On 28 August they provided area cover with 130 Squadron while troop concentrations at the Seine-crossing in Rouen were bombed. This was the longest duration operational flight ever undertaken by Mk. XIIs. Later that afternoon No. 41 Squadron found itself escorting Halifaxes to Cap Gris Nez and flew a third operation in the evening covering pathfinders marking for a Halifax raid. Bomber escorts continued to the end of August.

Intelligence reports were already indicating that the enemy was about to open his long-range V-2 rocket campaign. The question was—from where would the rockets be launched? A concentrated effort was made to find the launching sites. Three armed reconnaissances to find the rocket launching sites were flown by No. 41 Squadron on 1 September, mainly over north-east France. Others followed on the next three days, then they were halted by bad weather. It was 9 September before the squadron was off again, this time to Holland, searching around Katwijk, The Hague, Rotterdam and Walcheren for V-2 sites and targets of opportunity. Next day another *Ranger* was flown, to Bruges and the Dutch islands, then a bomber escort was undertaken to the Breskens ferry, and more *Rhubarbs* followed. The task of trying to locate the V-2 bases was continued on 12 September, by which time there was no doubt that these lay around The Hague. Six Spitfire XIIs flew at low level to the Dutch coast, climbed near The Hague and headed north in search of the small, carefully concealed launching sites. Some pin-points were investigated without success until a site was found one and a half miles north of Katwijk.

When the squadron arrived back over their base and broke for landing they could see that their first Spitfire XIVs were on the airfield. But the work of the Mk. XIIs was not yet quite complete. Location of V-2 sites was essential, for only by destroying these could rocket attacks be halted. It was believed at this time that the rockets had some form of radio guidance. An attempt to ascertain whether this was true was now made by Fortresses of No. 214 Squadron, 100 Group. During the afternoon of 12 September, Fortress HB803:BU-L was sent to take up station off Holland and to make a radio search of the area. The patrol extended from 12.50 hours to 17.40 hours. Initially six Spitfire XIIs of No. 41 Squadron escorted the Fortress before landing at base at 16.05 hours. Three more joined the escort during mid-afternoon then, at 15.20 hours, Flg. Off. D. E. Tebbitt in MD850 and Flt. Sgt. I. T. Stevenson in MB858 took off to make the final Mk. XII operational sorties again escorting the Fortress, before landing at their base at 17.25 hours. The operational career of the Spitfire XII was completed.

Transfer to second-line duty was rapid. In late September 1944 fourteen Spitfire XIIs were delivered to the Fighter Leaders' School at Milfield, but their usefulness was limited and they were withdrawn late October 1944. After months in maintenance units eight Mk. XIIs were released to No. 595 Anti-Aircraft Co-operation Squadron, Aberporth, where they remained for army support duties until the autumn.

Post-war use was very limited. Several examples were placed in the hands of the Air Training Corps, the last example extant probably being MB798 which was held by No. 93 A.T.C. Squadron between March 1946 and November 1949.

The part played by the Spitfire XII in the overall Spitfire story lay far beyond its own usefulness for from it stemmed the most refined Spitfires. It was in the Spitfire XII that the Rolls-Royce Griffon engine—still in front-line service in the Shackleton A.E.W.2—was introduced to service.

Spitfire XII—main characteristics

Wing

Span 32 ft. 7 in. Aerofoil section NACA 2200. Mean chord 7 ft. 1 in. Wing incidence 2°. Wing dihedral 6°. Wing area including flaps and ailerons 231 sq. ft. Total area of ailerons 18·9 sq. ft. Total area of flaps 15·6 sq. ft.
Universal Wing as fitted to the Spitfire Vc, but with tips clipped. Armament restricted to 2 × 20 mm. Hispano cannon Mk. I or II and 4 × ·303 in. Browning machine guns. Cannon belt fed with 120 r.p.g. Machine guns 350 r.p.g.
Wheel track 5 ft. 8½ in. Tailwheel fixed on early aircraft.

Fuselage (with special attachments at Frame 5 for the Griffon engine)

Length 31 ft. 10 in. Height to tip of propeller—tail down 11 ft.
Height to centre of propeller boss 7 ft. 3 in.
Height to wing tips—tail down 5 ft. 4 in.
Height to tip of tail fin 6 ft. 9 in.
Maximum fuselage width 3 ft. 6 in.
Tailplane span over elevators 10 ft. 6 in.
Tailplane maximum chord 4 ft.
Tailplane area including elevators 31·46 sq. ft.

Propeller

Four-bladed Rotol Type R13/4F/SB Dural with 35° pitch or Type R13/405/6 Jablo constant speed.

Fuel tankage

Early aircraft upper 48 gal., lower 37 gal.
Later aircraft upper 36 gal., lower 49 gal.

Oil tankage

Early aircraft 6 gal., later aircraft 7 gal.

Engine

Rolls-Royce Griffon IV maximum power output for take off 1,720 b.h.p. at 2,750 r.p.m. with +12 lb. sq. in. boost at sea level. In 'M' gear 1,735 b.h.p. at 2,750 r.p.m. with +12 sq. in. boost at 1,000 ft. In 'S' gear 1,495 b.h.p. at 2,750 r.p.m. at 14,500 ft.

Weights

Tare 5,580 lb., fuel and oil 675 lb., service load 825 lb., pilot 200 lb., gross weight 7,300 lb., overload weight 7,400 lb.

Range

At 263 m.p.h. at 20,000 ft.: with 85 gal. fuel load 329 st. ml.; with 115 gal. fuel load (including 30 gal. slipper tank) 493 st. ml.; ranges in still air.

Enemy aircraft claimed during engagement by Spitfire XIIs

Date	Pilot	Sqn.	Acft.	Details
17. 4.43	Flg. Off. R. Hogarth	41	EN235	Ju 88 off Ostend, 20.30 hours
23. 4.43	Flt. Lt. T. R. Poynton	41	EN601	Uncertain, Dieppe area, 11.20 hours
27. 4.43	Flg. Off. C. R. Birbeck	41	EN608	Uncertain, Somme area
3. 5.43	Sgt. W. L. East	41	EN612	Uncertain, Dieppe area
25. 5.43	Sqn. Ldr. R. H. Harries	91	EN625	2 Bf 109 ⎫
25. 5.43	Flt. Lt. J. Maridor	91	MB832	1 Bf 109 ⎪
25. 5.43	Flg. Off. G. W. Bond	91	MB805	1 Bf 109 ⎬ off Folkestone 21.52 hours
25. 5.43	Flg. Off. J. Round	91	EN624	1 Bf 109 ⎪
25. 5.43	Plt. Off. D. H. Davy	91	EN623	1 Bf 109 ⎪
4. 6.43	Flg. Off. J. Solack	41	MB800	1 Bf 109 ⎭
6. 6.43	Plt. Off. D. H. Davy	91	MB820	1 Fw 190 off Le Treport
16. 6.43	Flg. Off. V. P. Seydel	91	EN627	1 Fw 190, EN627 FTR
16. 6.43	Flg. Off. R. S. Nash	91	EN625	1 Fw 190 in Channel
18. 7.43	Wg. Cdr. R. H. Harries	91	MB831	2 Bf 109 Poix area
24. 8.43	Flg. Off. Stenborg	91	MB805 ⎫	
24. 8.43	Flt. Sgt. Mulcany	91	EN618 ⎬ 1 Bf 109 shared, near Beaumont	
24. 8.43	Flg. Off. W. G. Mart	91	EN620 ⎭	
2. 9.43	Flt. Lt. I. G. Matthews	91	EN604	1 Bf 109 in sea off Le Touquet
2. 9.43	Flg. Off. G. W. Bond	91	EN614	1 Bf 109 in sea off Le Touquet
4. 9.43	Sqn. Ldr. N. A. Kynaston	91	MB803	1 Fw 190 nr. Le Touquet
4. 9.43	Flg. Off. G. Stenborg	91	MB805	1 Fw 190 nr. Le Touquet
4. 9.43	Flt. Lt. C. R. Birbeck	41	EN608	1 Fw 190 nr. Le Touquet
8. 9.43	Flt. Sgt. R. Blumer	91	EN620	1 Fw 190 Lille area
8. 9.43	Plt. Off. C. R. Fraser	91	MB854	1 Fw 190
16. 9.43	Flg. Off. B. Newman	41	MB857	1 Fw 190 Beaumont area
16. 9.43	Sqn. Ldr. N. A. Kynaston	91	MB803	2 Fw 190 Beamont area
16. 9.43	Flg. Off. J. Andrieux	91	MB839	1 Bf 109G Beaumont area
16. 9.43	Flt. Lt. G. Stenborg	91	MB805	1 Fw 190 Beaumont area
19. 9.43	Wg. Cdr. R. H. Harries	41	MB839	1 Fw 190 Lille area
19. 9.43	Flt. Lt. J. C. Doll	91	MB851	1 Fw 190 Lille area
22. 9.43	Wg. Cdr. R. H. Harries	41	MB836	1 Fw 190 Evreux area
22. 9.43	Flg. Off. B. B. Newman	41	MB857	1 Fw 190 Evreux area
22. 9.43	Flg. Off. C. R. Birbeck	41	EN608	1 Fw 190 Spitfire FTR
22. 9.43	Flg. Off. D. H. Smith	41	MB843	1 Fw 190 (probable) Evreux area
23. 9.43	Sqn. Ldr. N. A. Kynaston	91	MB803	1 Fw 190 Beauvais area
23. 9.43	Flt. Lt. J. C. Doll	91	MB842	1 Fw 190 Beauvais area
23. 9.43	Flg. Off. G. Stenborg	91	EN620	1 Bf 109 Beauvais area
24. 9.43	Flt. Lt. A. A. Glen	41	MB801	2 Fw 190 Beauvais area
24. 9.43	Flg. Off. E. Galitzine	41	MB838	1 Fw 190 (probable) Beauvais area

24. 9.43 Sqn. Ldr. N. A. Kynaston	91	MB803 1 Fw 190 Beauvais area	
24. 9.43 Flt. Lt. J. C. Doll	91	MB842 1 Fw 190 Beauvais area	
24. 9.43 Flt. Lt. J. P. Maridor	91	MB849 1 Fw 190 Beauvais area	
24. 9.43 Flg. Off. A. G. O'Shaughnessy	41	MB836 1 Fw 190 Beauvais area	
24. 9.43 Flt. Lt. R. S. Easby	91	EN626 1 Bf 109 Beauvais area	
27. 9.43 WG. Cdr. R. H. Harries	91	EN618 1 Bf 109 Beauvais area	
18.10.43 Flg. Off. J. Andrieux	91	MB839 1 Bf 109G Beauvais area	
20.10.43 Wg. Cdr. R. H. Harries	41	MB836 2 Bf 109G	⎫
20.10.43 Flg. Off. B. Newman	41	MB858 1 Bf 109G	⎪
20.10.43 Flg. Off. P. Cowell	41	MB795 1 Fw 190	Fighter sweep
20.10.43 Flg. Off. R. Collis	41	MB850 1 Bf 109G	⎬
20.10.43 Sqn. Ldr. N. A. Kynaston	91	MB803 1 Fw 190	Rouen–Evreux
20.10.43 Flg. Off. J. C. Doll	91	MB842 1 Fw 190	area
20.10.43 Flg. Off. R. S. Nash	91	EN625 1 Bf 109G	⎪
20.10.43 Flt. Sgt. R. Blumer	91	MB833 1 Bf 109G	⎭

Notes on individual Spitfire XIIs

No. 41 Squadron aircraft

EN221 30.5.44–27.6.44; **EN224** 15.5.44–27.6.44; **EN226** 8.6.43–3, 16.6.44–FTR 28.8.44 from bomber escort; **EN227** 8.6.44–20.9.44; **EN228** 24.2.43–14.5.43, 24.7.44–20.9.44; **EN229** 13.3.43–17.5.43, 28.6.44–28.9.44; **EN231** 9.3.43–FTR 18.6.44 ditched, English Channel; **EN232** 9.5.43–28.5.43 crash landed Friston; **EN233** 28.2.43–FTR 18.7.43 from fighter sweep; **EN234** 4.3.43–20.11.43; **EN235** 2.3.43–FTR 18.7.43, shot down over France; **EN236** 7.3.43–27.8.43, 3.9.43–?. 9.43; **EN237** 11.3.43–13.3.44 crashed on take off; **EN238** 14.3.43–23.7.43, 26.6.44–20.9.44; **EN601** 14.3.43–FTR 23.4.43 from Dieppe area; **EN602** 14.3.43–20.12.43, 16.6.44–22.9.44; **EN603** 20.3.43–9.12.43; **EN604** 22.3.43–13.4.43 withdrawn after battle damage; **EN605** 22.3.43–23.9.44; **EN606** 23.3.43–16.6.43; **EN607** 22.3.43–27.4.43 damaged in combat; **EN608** 22.4.43–22.9.43, in the sea 20 miles south of Ford; **EN609** 22.3.43–26.9.43, 16.6.44–28.9.44; **EN610** 24.3.43–24.4.43 crashed nr. White Horse Inn, Canterbury Road, Hawkinge; **EN611** 30.3.43–27.8.43 in the sea; **EN612** 30.3.43–FTR 3.5.43, shot down by Fw 190 on Dieppe patrol; **EN615** 2.8.44–20.9.44; **EN619** 27.4.44–28.9.44; **EN620** 14.3.44–4.6.44; **EN622** 27.7.44–FTR 3.9.44 from armed reconnaissance, Holland; **EN625** 15.9.44–20.9.44; **MB794** 29.9.43–FTR 9.6.44 from beachhead patrol; **MB795** 29.9.43–15.9.44; **MB796** 21.5.43–FTR 6.9.43 caught fire, abandoned; **MB797** 22.8.43–12.2.44 crash landed Harty Marshes, Sheppey; **MB798** 14.9.43–22.9.43; **MB799** 14.9.43–16.9.43; **MB800** 19.5.43–FTR 19.9.43, shot down by Fw 190; **MB801** 11.5.43–20.11.43 crashed; **MB802** 11.5.43–FTR 24.9.43, shot down by FW 190; **MB803** 15.5.44–21.6.44; **MB804** 22.8.43–16.7.44 damaged in action; **MB829** 13.5.43–3.5.44; **MB830** 2.10.43–23.6.44 damaged in action; **MB831** 13.8.44–1.9.44 shot down on armed reconnaissance, Holland; **MB834** 1.6.43–FTR 3.10.43, crashed at sea; **MB836** 26.6.44–28.9.44; **MB837** 1.9.43–8.7.44 damaged by disintegrating V-1; **MB838** 19.8.43–15.11.43; **MB840** 19.10.43–20.9.44; **MB841** 15.5.44–18.7.44; **MB842** 7.3.44–FTR 12.6.44, crashed in Channel; **MB843** 1.9.43–FTR 2.6.44, in the sea north of Herm Island, C.Is.; **MB844** 18.8.43–11.12.43; **MB845** 20.7.43–4.6.44; **MB846** 20.7.43–1.12.43 damaged in action; **MB847** 20.7.43–21.6.44; **MB850** 29.9.43–20.10.43, 24.7.44–20.9.44; **MB853** 17.7.44–20.9.44; **MB854** ?.?.?–17.8.44, 24.11.44–8.1.45; **MB856** 23.6.44–9.9.44 damaged on a *Ranger* to Holland; **MB858** 7.9.43–15.12.44; **MB860** ?.7.44–15.12.44; **MB861** 21.7.44–?.?.44; **MB862** 7.8.43–20.9.44; **MB863** 26.11.43–20.3.44 crashed, overshot Friston; **MB875** 23.6.44–25.8.44 crashed taking off from Lympne; **MB876** 15.5.44–FTR 18.6.44; **MB877** 28.5.44–17.7.44 collided with Tiger Moth DE575 during take off; **MB878** 14.7.44–28.9.44; **MB880** 14.12.43–FTR 17.8.44, crashed in Channel, fuel shortage; **MB881** 21.12.43–7.6.44 damaged on *Rhubarb*; **MB882** 21.12.43–20.9.44.

No. 91 Squadron aircraft

EN222 4.3.43–25.3.44; **EN223** 20.11.43–6.1.44; **EN227** 29.12.43–28.1.44 damaged by EN606 when latter was landing and written off; **EN229** 4.3.44–20.3.44; **EN230** 24.5.43–1.9.43 written off; **EN234** 20.11.43–9.3.44; **EN602** 20.3.44; **EN230** 24.5.43–1.9.43 written off; **EN234** 20.11.43–9.3.44; **EN602** Forest Row, East Grinstead; **EN606** 29.9.43–20.1.44 crashed into EN277 on landing at Tangmere; **EN613** 22.4.43–31.1.44 crashed in Channel; **EN614** 1.5.43–FTR 19.9.43, shot down into sea off Dunkirk; **EN615** 1.5.43–28.1.44; **EN617** 29.5.43–FTR 16.9.43, shot down 12 miles west of Le Hay; **EN618** 7.5.43–31.1.44 in the sea; **EN619** 1.5.43–24.10.43; **EN620** 13.5.43–14.3.44; **EN621** 13.5.43–5.2.44 crashed at Reigate Hill, Surrey; **EN622** 13.5.43–6.6.43, 17.2.44–2.4.44; **EN623** 9.5.43–9.3.44; **EN624** 13.5.43–23.1.44 crashed; **EN625** 13.5.43–9.3.44; **EN626** 27.9.43–6.11.43 crashed east of Horsham; **EN627** 13.5.43–FTR 16.6.43, shot down SE of Dover; **MB799** 16.9.43–19.9.43 in the sea off Ramsgate; **MB803** 13.5.43–23.10.43, 28.10.43–6.11.43 crashed; **MB803** 16.5.43–fate unknown; **MB830** 17.5.43–2.10.43; **MB831** 17.5.43–25.10.43; **MB832** 16.5.43–6.6.43, 3.1.44–FTR 23.1.44; **MB833** 8.6.43–12.6.44 written off; **MB835** ?.5.43–FTR 16.6.43, shot down in Channel; **MB836** 22.8.43–20.3.44; **MB839** 11.6.43–9.3.44; **MB841** 9.10.43–15.5.44; **MB842** 19.6.43–24.9.43 damaged in action; **MB848** 15.6.43–18.3.44; **MB849** 2.9.43–8.4.44 crashed at Gloucester Hill, Amble, Northumberland; **MB851** ?.8.43–FTR 8.9.43, shot down, Lille area; **MB857** 20.2.44–?.3.44; **MB859** 9.11.43–6.12.43 mid-air collision with EN604 over Forest Row, East Grinstead; **MB860** 22.1.44–20.3.44; **MB861** 1.2.44–20.3.44; **MB876** 29.9.43–15.5.44; **MB877** 29.9.43–?.?.44; **MB879** 6.12.43–9.12.44.

No. 595 Squadron

EN224 14.5.45–29.7.45; **EN605** 19.5.45–29.7.45; **EN623** 15.6.45–26.6.45 ditched in Newquay Bay, Cardigan; **MB798** 2.5.45–2.9.45; **MB804** 3.5.45–2.9.45; **MB837** 14.5.45–1.11.45; **MB845** 28.4.45–17.12.45; **MB848** 29.12.44–31.7.45; **MB862** ?.5.45–22.11.45.

Fighter Leaders' School, Milfield

EN227 20.9.44–19.10.44; **EN228** 20.9.44–26.10.44; **EN229** 28.9.44–28.10.44; **EN238** 20.9.44–26.10.44; **EN608** 28.9.44–26.10.44; **EN615** 20.9.44–31.10.44; **EN619** 20.9.44–26.10.44; **EN625** 20.9.44–19.10.44; **MB836** 28.9.44–26.10.44; **MB840** 20.9.44–26.10.44; **MB850** 20.9.44–16.11.44; **MB853** 20.9.44–19.10.44–2.8.45–28.2.46; **MB878** 28.9.44–26.10.44; **MB880** 20.9.44–29.10.44.

Used for experimental and trials purposes

EN221 A & AEE 5.11.42–19.2.43, Tangmere 5.10.44–29.10.44; **EN222** A & AEE 5.12.42–3.3.43, AFDU 24.5.43–4.3.44;**EN223** AFDU 21.12.42–26.6.43, 10.11.43–20.11.43; **EN224** CRD VA 15.12.42–13.2.43; **EN225** Handling Sqn., Hullavington 24.12.42–1.12.43; AFDU 4.1.45–10.7.45; **EN226** CRD VA Chattis Hill 29.1.43–8.6.43; **EN227** CRD VA Chattis Hill 1.2.43–28.2.43; AFDU/CFE 19.10.44–4.10.45; **EN230** AFDU 13.2.43–24.5.43; **EN616** CRD RR 6.5.43–29.3.45; **EN625** AFDU 19.10.44–11.12.44 crashed in Norfolk; **MB853** AFDU 19.10.44–2.8.45.

Prototype history, DP845

CRD VA 31.12.41, A & AEE 10.9.42, CRD VA, A & AEE 5.6.43, VA Worthy Down 11.8.43, VA Castle Bromwich 11.10.45, VA High Post 13.10.45, MPRD Cowley 4.10.46 and scrapped.

Notes on miscellaneous users of Mk. XIIs

EN224 to College of Aeronautics, Cranfield 4.7.46; **EN234** Old Sarum 14.3.45–17.8.45 crashed while performing aerobatics; **EN238** to No. 1 School of Technical Training, Halton, as 567OM 19.9.45, reduced to scrap 28.4.47; **EN607** CRD Malcolm Ltd. 14.2.44–13.6.44; **EN615** Empire Air Armament School Manby 15.12.44–3.8.45; **MB798** to 93 ATC Sqn 12.3.46, struck off charge 30.11.49; **MB795** became 4875M, struck off charge 1.1.48; **MB803** used by 61 OTU ?.?.44 to 15.5.44; **MB838** to 5921M at 538 Sqn ATC 12.3.46, struck off charge 28.3.47; **MB844** E.A.A.S. Manby 14.12.44–3.8.45; **MB844** became 5922M with 77 Sqn. ATC 12.3.46, struck off charge 6.11.47; **MB851** 41 Group Comm. Flt. Old Sarum 27.8.45–20.8.46; **MB855** CRD Malcolm Ltd., White Waltham 31.12.43–12.3.44, E.A.A.S. 14.12.44–3.8.45, to 487 Sqn. ATC as 5923M and struck off charge in June 1946; **MB856** to 4 Sqn. ATC 21.9.44–30.4.45.

Part Two

The Armstrong Whitworth Albemarle: An Unwanted Aeroplane

Victory fires blazed throughout Britain on VE-Day 1945, and in Cambridge the inhabitants warmed to a tremendous blaze on Midsummer Common. Much of the glow glared from plywood and fabric of many a hue, remnants of a controversial British wartime aircraft, for remains of Albemarle transports had arrived from Marshall's Flying School for burning. It was a symbolic funeral pyre at the moment of victory, all but the finale to a sombre story.

The Royal Air Force fought the first few years of the 1939–45 war with aircraft whose design requirements were cast in the mid-1930s. Before war commenced, specifications had been laid down for second-generation machines which, it was hoped, would join squadrons in 1940. Tremendous demands made upon the aircraft industry were paralleled by the corresponding need for resources and materials, many of which originated overseas, making them vulnerable to attack as they crossed the oceans *en route* for Britain. Apart from the need for vast numbers of airframes, there was also a requirement for many engines, and it was feared that manufacturers might be unable to cope with the demand.

All aircraft manufacturers were involved in the expansion schemes, and by 1939 they were producing the range of aeroplanes prescribed in the mid-1930s, but the newer types intended for replacement of interim types such as the Wellington, Hampden and Spitfire were not ready for production when the war commenced. What the Air Ministry and Air Staff did not plan for was repeated modification of existing designs and aircraft, which in some cases made protracted production a worthwhile venture. These points need to be kept in mind when considering the unfortunate Albemarle.

An attractive solution for expansion of aircraft production lay with the idea of utilizing the capacity of Dominion sources. Another was to buy from the Americans, although their aircraft were considered too inferior for front-line use. Both plans posed supply problems, especially when it was realized that overseas production of British designs would inevitably require shipment of power plants from Britain. Fitting American engines was a possibility, the alternative to which was the shipping of airframes to Britain where the power plants would be installed. In these cases vulnerable loads would be committed to ocean attack.

A third possibility manifested itself late in 1937—the construction of aircraft from materials indigenous to Britain, or of those which would not be in short supply. This meant a mixture of wood and metal. Such an idea was not new in itself since many aircraft had been built of composite construction employing steel tubing and wood, but what was new was the involvement of companies outside the aircraft industry, in particular manufacturers of wooden furniture, to manufacture large sub-assemblies. The Air Staff was, from the outset, sceptical as to the viability of such a scheme. Wooden construction seemed a retrogressive step where combat aircraft were concerned and was considered suitable only for training-aircraft. Even when the superlative Mosquito was mooted—involving similar concepts to the 1937 suggestion—suspicious voices were raised against it simply because it was not of metal construction. However, by late 1937, ideas for composite construction, coupled with employment of firms outside the aircraft industry, had won ministerial favour. It was suggested that an experimental aircraft be built.

Planning, design and production

Time was short, as international events indicated a need for as many combat aircraft as possible. In the closing weeks of 1937 a specification had been drawn up by Air Ministry Research and Development for an experimental aeroplane. This was now quickly evolved into a specification for a twin-engined bomber designed to be rapidly built, and of composite metal and wood construction. It needed to be simply constructed in order that largely untrained and unskilled labour could be utilized. The production philosophy had much in common with that applicable to the aircraft's design—to enlarge the base from which rapid expansion of aircraft-production capacity would be achieved in order to meet wartime demands. Details were to be made using material not generally in demand by the aircraft industry. Similarly, with production, almost exclusive use would be made of the light engineering and wood-working industries for component production. Final assembly and flight testing would be the direct responsibility of the aircraft industry.

The Air Ministry (not, be it noted, the Air Staff) asked in their Specification B.9/38 of January 1938 for use of a composite structure of wood, metal and synthetic materials and pressed laminated wood. They appreciated that a weight penalty would arise, which came to be underestimated by the aircraft designers; a penalty which was to be met by clean aerodynamic form and the very smooth finish obtainable by using wood. The machine, they stated, must be suitable for day and night operations at home and overseas. Despite its construction it was to be suitable for maintenance in the open. Good load-carrying qualities, strong tail defence and wide load/fuel variations were prescribed.

The Air Ministry envisaged a maximum speed of not less than 300 m.p.h. at 15,000 ft. with a normal load, a demanding figure for a bomber at this time. A range of 1,500 miles at normal loading would follow a 500 yd. take-off run. The latter was to be limited because it was feared that airfield dimensions needed to be restricted for internal political reasons. Anything over 500 yards was looked upon as disturbing. For normal range a minimum bomb load of 1,500 lb. was required. A maximum load of not less than 3,000 lb. of bombs would match a long take off of 700 yd. and 2,000 miles range at 15,000 ft. For this there seemed no alternative to a long run. At normal loading, service ceiling was to be at least 28,000 ft. The machine should be able to fly easily on one engine at 10,000 ft. Specified crew numbered four—two pilots (one acting as navigator/bomb aimer), a radio operator and a gunner. There was to be accommodation for another pilot and extra radio operator on long flights.

In the tail would be the inevitable gun turret, whose gunner would be able to take his place from within the aircraft, and there was a suggestion for remotely controlled guns too. The 3,000 lb. bomb load would comprise 12×250 lb. or 6×500 lb. H.E. bombs and, in special overload state, $2 \times 2,000$ lb. A.P. bombs on special carriers. Secondary to performance was the best possible view for the pilot, navigator/bomb aimer and air gunner. The pilot was to have a good rear view, this an alternative for someone by his side.

Manoeuvrability was less important, but the aircraft should be able to dive bomb, possibly with its flaps reducing its speed. The bomb aimer would work from a seated position in the nose with the navigator close to the pilot. The fuselage was to be planned to enable the crew to move from station to station. Since it was envisaged that positioning flights might keep the aircraft aloft for fourteen hours some soundproofing was needed, and light, removable seats for additional crew were to be provided.

From the start the Air Staff had misgivings about the whole affair, for a bomber was being specified for which no operational requirement existed. They were consulted, and impressed upon Air Ministry R & D that the aircraft must have a hull able to accommodate heavy bombs—and that a tail turret was essential. They also pointed out the need to carry flame floats and flares for possible reconnaissance purposes.

In March 1938 both the Bristol Aeroplane Company and Armstrong Whitworth Aircraft tendered to the specification, while the Air Staff pressed the point that rapid construction would be essential. To them the machines were worth considering only as experimental aircraft. They felt that if either design proved successful, pressure would be brought upon them to agree to large-scale production; indeed, there was already talk of this. Air Ministry R & D were adamant that either machine, if chosen for production, should be built by firms outside the aircraft industry. In early conversations with the manufacturers the Air Staff laid down criteria which must be met by the aircraft, but it was clear that reconciling it to future needs was unattractive. In the Air Staff's opinion the aircraft should go forward, if it must, not as a bomber but as a general reconnaissance aircraft. For this reason Robert Saundby, Deputy Director of Operational Requirements, now argued that the standing specification should be cancelled. The Chief of the Air Staff did not entirely agree. He wanted 100 examples ordered of either a bomber or reconnaissance design.

The Deputy Chief of the Air Staff came forward in favour of experimenting with composite construction, pointing out that Air Ministry R & D had plans only for an experimental aircraft. An Air Staff specification for a useful type that could rapidly be produced in wartime, and which could regularly be updated according to need, could follow. Although, perhaps, of lower performance than might seem desirable, it would usefully augment the aircraft force potentially planned. A simple general reconnaissance type would have been preferable for experimental purposes to an aircraft for a bomber role for which an extensive projected force had already been laid down. Such a machine would not need strong defensive armament, whereas a bomber would need this coupled with high performance. In the Deputy Chief of the Air Staff's view there should be a test only of the practicability of producing an aircraft of composite materials which would be built by other than the main aircraft manufacturers, not a test of a front-line machine. By May 1938 the requirement had gradually evolved into one for a reconnaissance-bomber for rapid production, not merely a bomber of fairly advanced type.

Major J. Lloyd of Armstrong Whitworth submitted his proposals first, early in March 1938. The result of his work was a pleasant surprise to the Ministry. He proposed extensive use of steel tubing and compressed wood for the structure. Although this would not be a wooden aeroplane, considerable amounts of wood were to be used. It was clear that a good emergency aeroplane could be evolved. J. S. Buchanan, Deputy Director of Technical Development, wanted to press ahead with the placing of prototype orders by the end of March 1938. It was suggested at this time that Merlin RM 2SM (Merlin II with two-speed blowers), with the possible provision for Hercules III engines, be fitted to the aircraft.

At the end of March 1938 the R & D Department raised the question of armament. They were not in favour of a tail turret, but if the Air Staff insisted were prepared to ask for a two-gun tail turret. R & D preferred a four-gun dorsal turret with good all-round field of fire. They considered that an American-type gun blister might be useful to cover the lower field, and in their opinion the best defence for this aeroplane against attack from below was for it to 'hedge hop', advanced thinking indeed. In their opinion a tail turret would snatch 15 m.p.h. from the top speed, and complicate building. Furthermore, they considered that the Air Staff should accept a 2,000 lb. bomb load, and that bombs of up to only 500 lb. should be carried.

In April 1938 Air Ministry R & D expressed the view that some requirements ran contrary to the decisions of 12 January 1938 when it was agreed that the aircraft should have a bomb load of 1,000 lb. for 1,500 miles. The Chief of the Air Staff had made it clear that he thought a tail turret was needed and that a ventral dustbin turret should not be installed. The original concept had been for a simple and necessary aeroplane to replace the Blenheim. What was now being ordered was already a complicated and large aeroplane that seemed likely to be built only by existing aircraft builders. In his reply, the Chief of the Air Staff said that he did not recall any decision for a 1,000 lb. load, for this hardly seemed worth following up. Four men to deliver 1,000 lb. seemed wasteful. He considered the four-gun turret tail essential, and would not agree to abandoning this. He also felt it easier to include than a large dorsal turret and possibly an under blister. He agreed to a 1,500-mile range.

On 10 June 1938 Air Ministry R & D finally agreed with what the Air Staff had been saying, but reiterated that a 1,000 lb. load for 1,500 miles had been agreed. The new draft specification now being assembled improved upon the original ideas, which had been for two prototypes of a much smaller machine which was not mainly viewed as a general reconnaissance aircraft. At Armstrong Whitworth the mock-up of B.9/38 was now well advanced. Twin-Merlins were forecast as giving a speed of 320 m.p.h. at 20,000 ft. and a range of 1,500 miles with a 1,500 lb. bomb load.

In a further letter of 17 June the Deputy Chief of the Air Staff pointed out that he considered it unreasonable to expect an efficient bomber for 1939–40 service to be built of composite construction, but that the original specification had been drawn up to see what the industry could offer. Now, after months of discussion, it was decided to cancel B.9/38 and in its place prepare two similar specifications for a composite construction machine, a reconnaissance bomber, to Specifications 17/38 and 18/38.

The Bristol Aeroplane Company tendered to 17/38. Their scheme was discussed at Filton on 15 June 1938, the Deputy Director of Technical Development explaining that the original proposal had been for an experimental aircraft for rapid production, but that during 1938 this had evolved into one for a bomber-reconnaissance aeroplane which Bristol were now considering. The Deputy Director Operational Requirements then told the company that their proposals fell short of Air Staff needs, and that their design was only acceptable as a general reconnaissance aircraft. One may surmise that the company were disappointed, because they must have hoped that a Blenheim replacement, which was always to elude them, might be at hand. In his reply Mr. L. G. Frise stated that the performance of the Type 155 powered by two Bristol Taurus engines was bound up with the type of undercarriage adopted, and that if the normal tailwheel type was decided upon then the wing-loading would be about 27–30 lb./sq. ft. If a nosewheel type was fitted—then regarded as quite *avant garde*—the wing-loading would be higher. Approximate figures for the project were: wing area 720 sq. ft., wing span 70 ft., top speed about 320 m.p.h. at 15,000 ft. for the latter configuration, whereas with a tailwheel undercarriage the wing area would be about 890 sq. ft., wing span 80 ft. and top speed just over 300 m.p.h. But to the Ministry representatives the nosewheel layout appeared to be a gamble, and since the aircraft was somewhat experimental anyway it would be best not to complicate it.

The firm agreed, and a tailwheel layout was decided upon which would lead to a landing run of about 600 yards. Increased loadings were less likely to arise if the aircraft was to be a reconnaissance type. An offensive load of 1,000 lb. for 1,500 miles was agreed, with future provision for loads up to 10×250 lb. bombs, 8×500 lb. bombs or $2 \times 2,000$ lb. bombs, with tankage for a range of up to 3,000 miles. The largest bombs would partly protrude from the bomb bay, but to penalize the aircraft by having fairings to cover them would be unfair to the project. It was then agreed that Hercules SM engines with two-stage blowers would be installed. Dorsal and ventral turrets would be fitted and it was argued that their field of fire would cover almost all of the upper and lower hemispheres. The crew would number five—two pilots (one acting as navigator/bomb aimer), a radio operator and two gunners. Tropical operation must be possible even though the aircraft would have a plywood covering. Synthetic resin glue would fasten the wood to the structure without intervening fabric.

Basic planning, then, was complete for the B.17/38, a rugged machine which could easily be built by Bristol. High cruising speed, long endurance and good load-carrying capability with ready interchange of loads and adequate self-defence would characterize it.

A week later a proposal from Armstrong Whitworth, for a more ambitious design to B.18/38, was discussed at Whitley. Again, the firm's tender was said to fall short of the official requirements. Design work was ordered to proceed on a general reconnaissance aircraft which would have provision for bombing. It must carry a crew of five, a 1,500 lb. bomb load for a range of 2,000 miles and have a maximum ferry range—without bombs—of 4,000 miles. This meant that it would be slightly larger than the Bristol aeroplane. Bomb racks should cater for up to a 4,500 lb. load embracing 9×500 lb., 15×250 lb., 6×250 lb. 'B' bombs or $2 \times 2,000$ lb. bombs. Following an inspection of the firm's armament mock-up it was decided to opt for a four-gun dorsal turret and a two-gun retractable ventral turret, both being accessible from the forward part of the fuselage. A good view for the undergunner, acting as an observer when his turret was retracted, was called for. This led to a generous glazed portion beneath the extreme rear of the fuselage.

The agreed design was to go forward with Hercules engines in the first prototype and Merlins in the second, with the forthcoming Armstrong Siddeley Deerhound as a later alternative to the Hercules. It was estimated that the Hercules prototype would be ready in May 1939, the Merlin machine one month later.

Armstrong Whitworth had, however, laid out a high-wing-loading design around twin-Merlins. It would have a 3,500 lb. bomb load and a range of 2,500 miles, the wing-loading of about 38 lb./sq. ft. taking into account a nosewheel undercarriage chosen to improve ground handling. Redesign to incorporate the favoured air-cooled Hercules engines would increase all-up weight, compensated for by a smaller bomb load and fuel tankage. The original choice of Merlin engines had been made following their adoption for later Whitleys, but the Air Staff preferred air-cooled engines for long-range bombers. It was then agreed that the wing span would increase from 61 ft. to 67 ft. which increased the area by about 15 per cent to give a lower wing-loading of about 30 lb./sq. ft. This would then permit some changes during the development period.

From the start, the Air Staff, as will be recalled, were unwilling partners. Now the Air Force had to look forward to two aircraft, neither of which it wanted. In July 1938 a further reappraisal of the entire programme was undertaken. As a result it was decided that the Armstrong Whitworth machine was likely to be the better of the two. B.17/38 was therefore cancelled, allowing Bristol to devote themselves to other designs. The B.18/38 was to be built mainly of steel tubing and wood with a minimum of light alloy, thereby conserving a commodity that might soon be in short supply. Design of the type was to be arranged for ease of manufacture and to be laid out in a manner allowing sub-assemblies to be easily dismantled and carried on standard sixty-foot trailers. Construction of steel tubing with gusset plate joints was basic, the fuselage and wing to be plywood covered. Clearly an experienced aircraft firm would need to undertake final assembly and test-flying. The choice was ultimately narrowed down to Gloster Aircraft which was then part of the Hawker Group, of which Armstrong Whitworth was also a member.

Initially each component—front fuselage, wing centre section, etc.—was sub-contracted separately to each of two or three companies. While such features were not uncommon, especially during the late stages of the 1939–45 war, what was probably true only of the B.18/38 was that after building of the first two prototypes the parent company's responsibility was limited to design matters only. In retrospect it seems strange that this arrangement was so readily accepted. Few people seem to have appreciated, in advance, the almost inevitable difficulties and delays, leading automatically to high cost, which would be encountered. Tremendous effort would be required to train thousands of people in the special techniques involved with aircraft production. A situation soon arose in which no up-dated complete set of working drawings was available.

The general opinion in non-aircraft industrial circles was that any firm with years of experience in mass production of, for instance, motor cars, could switch to an aircraft component such as the B.18/38's wing (mainly metal) without undue difficulty. Some thought that they would teach the aircraft industry a thing or two about large-scale production. Similarly, any large furniture manufacturer should easily be capable of producing a wooden wing. What was not generally appreciated was an aircraft's fundamental requirement for the highest possible strength and stiffness. Weight ratios demanded carefully controlled workshop techniques and specialized materials, along with extensive and systematic inspection. Additionally, few furniture workers in 1940 had experience with resin-based adhesives.

On 18 August 1938, two prototypes of the B.18/38, P1360 and P1361, were ordered. At this time the projected performance would render the machine useful as either a bomber or general reconnaissance type, and design work and prototype construction would be the task of the Armstrong Whitworth works at Hamble, where production planning would take place before production was placed in the hands of others. Such divorce was to become a major blunder. The decision to free the major plant at Coventry of the Albemarle was made to ensure that Whitley work would not be interrupted.

Design work went ahead rapidly, during which time it was decided to fit Hercules engines to both prototypes. Progress was quite good and shortly before the war broke out it was decided to increase the initial order to 200 aircraft, a further 198 being eventually contracted for on 13 November 1939, these to be assembled by Gloster Aircraft at Brockworth. Delivery was to build up to sixty per month. It seemed that the aircraft would offer an excellent opportunity to bring into war work many production sources, so much so that there was a new decision to expand the order to 1,000 aircraft including the two prototypes. Gloster were to deliver the first example in October 1940, thirty-two per month by June 1941 and 100 per month by December with the help of the Yeadon works. In the event there was no space available at the latter and alternative arrangements were needed.

Placing the B.18/38 at Hamble freed Armstrong Whitworth to pursue other designs. In the summer of 1939 they produced their scheme in answer to Specification B.1/39, a four-Griffon or Deerhound bomber with cannon armament loosely based upon the configuration of the Albemarle, with a wing span of 104 ft. and a length of 85 ft. An adaptation of the huge dorsal cannon turret of the Boulton Paul P.92, planned for the R.5/39 flying-boat, was married to the design in a later stage of project definition. In October 1939 a high-speed bomber project was entertained, again with four Hercules, Merlins or Deerhounds and retaining heavy armament. This, the A.W.44, was designed with a nose turret and heavy cannon dorsal and ventral armament, a wing span of 83 ft. 6 in. and a length of 64 ft. 4 in. A projected twin-Merlin high-speed bomber, the A.W.45, with a wing span of 43 ft. and a length of 36 ft. 3 in. was also designed at this time and in 1940 the A.W.44 was adapted to Specification B.7/40. Thus, the parent company for B.18/38 was busily employed early in the war and had rather turned away from the A.W.41.

At the time of the first production order for B.18/38 the Air Staff had a major worry on their hands. Two aeroplanes which they had specified for short-range general reconnaissance, the Beaufort and the Botha, were both in trouble. Both were intended as torpedo bombers, there being a desperate need to replace the aged Vildebeest in Coastal Command. If the 18/38, for which the name Albemarle had now been chosen, was to serve as a general reconnaissance aircraft, it seemed logical that it should replace at least the troublesome Botha and become a torpedo bomber. There can be little doubt that the Albemarle went ahead with such an idea in the minds of some of the Air Staff, and the Air Ministry informed Armstrong Whitworth that it must make suitable modifications to the aircraft. This must have come as a shock to the company and they immediately replied that they had no experience with the design of torpedo bombers, which were looked upon as very specialized aircraft.

Notwithstanding, the Air Ministry repeated their request. They asked that the Albemarle be adapted to carry a torpedo under each mainplane instead of the possible 2,000 lb. smoke-curtain gear. However, it soon became apparent that in the only position possible the torpedo would foul the ailerons. One possibility was to alter the latter—very undesirable—and the other was to carry the torpedo in the belly, always assuming the undercarriage setting would permit this. The net outcome was that it was too late for such a radical change without almost total redesign.

The production run already agreed was clearly too small for a major type and

11.   P1360, the first prototype Albemarle, seen here with short-span wings and small-area fins and rudders in April 1940. It was eventually written off after a forced landing at Crewkerne, Somerset, on 4 February 1941

on 30 January a contract for a further 800 Albemarles was placed. At the same time it was decreed that the first 100 would have black-painted undersurfaces in night-bomber style. By April 1940 it had further been decided that the first 250 machines would be completed as bombers, after which would come the general reconnaissance examples for Coastal Command, easy to identify on account of their silver undersurfaces. Coastal Command would repaint any earlier aircraft transferred to them. The torpedo-bomber idea had been discarded.

The first prototype Albemarle was completed by February 1940 and first flew on 20 March. Taxiing trials revealed a serious problem, for it was immediately clear that the aircraft needed a very long take-off run even at the low weight of 26,500 lb. at which it was to begin flight trials. Early take offs were viewed with concern and it was clear that something must be done. The obvious solution lay in increased wing span needed to improve lift coefficient, although increased structure weight would occur. After a few exploratory flights P1360 was flown from Hamble to Baginton. The second prototype was taken there by road in July, mainly because work there would be less subject to possible enemy interference.

The take-off problem was serious and the whole future of the aircraft in jeopardy. The only possible solution, and the one accepted, was to increase the wing span by ten feet which meant scrapping parts already made for about a dozen machines, and also to build new jigs which meant delay. It was at this time, after the fall of France, that the Ministry of Aircraft Production was established and issued the edict that production would centre on six major aircraft types currently in production; work of an experimental nature would amount to little. Consequently there was further slippage in the Albemarle's career.

With the extended wings fitted, P1360's take-off trials were resumed on 28 September 1940 only to be halted on 30 September when the aircraft made a wheels-up landing incurring several weeks of slow repair. The resumption of flight trials showed that the take off was still not good and the performance below that forecast, for the increase in span had, of course, added to structure weight. Fins and rudders of increased area improved handling however. In mid-November 1940, P1360 proceeded to Boscombe Down for handling trials. Before these were completed P1360 was destroyed in a crash on 4 February 1941 after wing skinning became detached during flight. J. H. Hartley, one of the Albemarle flight-test observers recalls: 'This was an incident that became memorable. Deterioration of the plywood covering to the wing surface had set in and caused a large area to become detached in flight. The aircraft became uncontrollable and the order to bale out was given. A Bristol engine representative operated his parachute a little too soon and it became entangled with the tailplane. This, strangely enough, made the aircraft manoeuvrable again and it was subsequently force landed at Wootton Waven, near Leamington, with the unfortunate man still dangling from the tail.

'He managed to release himself moments before touchdown and his fall was cushioned by snow. He had received serious injuries, from which he ultimately recovered.' The aircraft was destroyed by fire soon after a wheels-up landing.

On 20 April 1941 the second prototype — P1361 — was first flown, this machine having a 77 ft. wing span. Pilots flying the aircraft knew for sure that as its loading increased it would take unacceptable runs to get airborne. At full load, it was suggested, it might never get off! So bad had the take-off run been with short wings that no official trials had even been contemplated.

In February 1941 it had been decided that the third to tenth aircrafts (already being built) must be modified to have increased span, after it had been initially suggested that these go forward for use as lightly loaded trainers. It looked as if even after modifications the Albemarle would never be of use at over 32,000 lb.; 3,000 lb. below the forecast all-up weight. In other words, Albemarles would never be able to carry the intended offensive load for the intended range. As early as mid-1940, after the initial flight trials, it had been reckoned that under maximum-range conditions it would be necessary to discard all bombs and 550 gallons of fuel, less the emergency load, to maintain height in the aircraft. Now, and even more worrying, it was coming into production and 1,000 were on order. A special organization, an offshoot of the Gloster Aeroplane Company, had come into being on 1 April 1941 to assemble and test these aircraft.

After a few flights the second prototype was moved to Boscombe Down, arriving there on 23 April 1941 for the resumption of official trials. Within a few days these were halted by the collapse of the nosewheel. An intensive provisional assessment had luckily been undertaken by then, although armament and navigation trials were incomplete.

The maximum possible take-off weight was assessed as 36,500 lb. and the take-off run in still air a worrying 1,240 yd. to clear 50 ft., about twice that specified. In the bomber role the machine weighed 23,800 lb. tare. Allowing 1,000 lb. for crew,

12.   P1361, the second prototype Albemarle, features extended wing span and enlarged tail unit. In the depicted form the Albemarle had a wing span of 77 ft., length of 59 ft. 11 in., height to propeller tip of 15 ft. 7 in., wing area 803.5 sq.ft., tailplane span 26 ft. 4 in. and tailplane area of 165.43 sq.ft.

5,540 lb. for fuel, 540 lb. for oil, 3,500 lb. bomb load and a movable military load of 2,190 lb., the all-up weight came to 36,570 lb. In the reconnaissance role the tare weight amounted to 23,800 lb., crew 1,000 lb., fuel 8,360 lb. (1,160 gal.), oil 850 lb. (94 gal.), auxiliary tanks and mountings 64 lb. and movable military load 1,850 lb.—total 35,924 lb. The flying qualities, however, were better than expected, and similar to those of the, then new, Hercules-powered Wellington III. The controls were rather better, but for the heavy elevators, and the view for the pilot was quite good except during early stages of landing approach when it was necessary to rock the aircraft from side to side for a view of the runway ahead. Landing was made easy by the nosewheel undercarriage layout, but the brakes heated rapidly.

It was longitudinally stable, but the aft c.g. limit was no better than that of the Wellington. Control layout was acceptable, the interior layout good with the well-glazed navigation station superior to contemporary bombers. Large expanses of glazing meant, however, that blackout might be a problem. Dual control was provided, an advance over the Wellington. Contact between crew stations was good, although the crew had to clamber over a midships fuselage tank.

The top speed was a disappointing 245–250 m.p.h. T.A.S. at 11,000/12,000 ft. The service ceiling was only 17,500 ft.; time to 15,000 ft. about 30 min. Cruising speed was 170–180 m.p.h. T.A.S. Range with 3,500 lb. bomb load was assessed as 1,300 miles, 975 miles for operational purposes allowing for take off and climb. With a 4,500 lb. load, range would fall to 790 miles in still air making normal allowances. It was reckoned to be about 2,060 miles for the reconnaissance version, 1,550 miles after making normal allowances. The maximum height at which the machine would fly on one engine was only 3,000 ft. and at only 28,000 lb. weight.

Some alarm was occasioned by the vibrating and rocking belly turret. Aim from it was impossible, and no other Albemarle was fitted with this feature. The Defiant-type dorsal turret seemed cramped, but was acceptable. In addition, weathering of the machine quickly turned out to be bad, so much so that it had to be kept in a hangar. There was alternate shrinkage and swelling of the ply covering of the fuselage, which opened at circumferential joints where strips were covered or butted, leaving rain to enter. An overlap joint was suggested, but wetting and drying caused the glue to dissolve and surfaces fell apart.

In August 1941, with the second prototype still under test after three and a half years of design and development, performance estimates for the production Albemarle 1 bomber were drawn up. These were closely akin to those of the Wellington, a type that the Albemarle would have replaced had all gone well. Its gross weight was assessed as 36,500 lb., top speed 260 m.p.h. T.A.S. at 14,000 ft. Cruising speed at 15,000 ft. would be 202 m.p.h. T.A.S. in M.S. gear, 220 m.p.h. T.A.S. in F.S. gear. The most economic speed seemed likely to be about 190–200 m.p.h. T.A.S. at 15,000 ft., service ceiling 18,500 ft., range 1,050 miles with 4,500 lb. bomb load and 1,700 miles with 1,500 lb. load. Like the second prototype, production machines would have Bristol Hercules XI engines giving 1,590 h.p. for take off and 1,460 h.p. at 9,000 ft. A comparison of performance with the Wellington II was undertaken showing these features:

Albemarle (Hercules XI)

(a) With 3,500 lb. bomb load: cruising speed 170 m.p.h. T.A.S. with a range of 1,300 miles. Fuel load 770 gal.

(b) With 1,800 lb. bomb load: cruising speed 215 m.p.h. T.A.S. with a range of 1,510 miles, and cruising speed 170 m.p.h. with a range of 1,820 miles. Fuel load 980 gal.

(c) With a 4,500 lb. bomb load: cruising speed 215 m.p.h. T.A.S. with a range of 1,050 miles at 10,000 ft. Fuel load 635 gal. Loaded weight was 36,500 lb., take-off run to clear 50 ft. obstacle was 1,240 yd. Service ceiling 17,500 ft. Maximum speed in this condition 250 m.p.h. T.A.S. at 11,500 ft.

(d) In reconnaissance role: cruising speed 170 m.p.h. T.A.S. with a range of 2,060 miles. All-up weight 35,924 lb.

Wellington II (Merlin X)

(a) With 3,500 lb. bomb load: cruising speed 195 m.p.h. T.A.S. with a range of 1,580 miles. Economic cruise speed 175 m.p.h. T.A.S. with a range of 1,725 miles. Fuel load 750 gal.

(b) With 1,150 lb. bomb load: cruising speed 195 m.p.h. T.A.S. with a range of 2,245 miles. Economic cruise speed 175 m.p.h. T.A.S. with a range of 2,445 miles. Fuel load 1,830 gal.

(c) With 4,500 lb. bomb load: cruising speed 195 m.p.h. T.A.S. with a range of 1,275 miles at 15,000 ft. Fuel load 614 gal. Loaded weight 32,000 lb., take-off run to clear 50 ft. obstacle was 1,350 yd. Service ceiling 18,000 ft. Maximum speed in this condition 244 m.p.h. T.A.S. at 17,000 ft.

By summer 1941 the Ministries were showing alarm at the slow production rate. Delivery had been scheduled to commence in June 1940: 100 examples to be delivered by the end of that year, 496 by the close of July 1941 and the remainder by January 1942. In fact by June 1941 only the two prototypes had been built. It looked, at that time, as if only forty Albemarles would be ready by the end of 1941, possibly 600 a year later—if production could be raised to fifty per month—and 1,000 by June 1943. By that time the Albemarle would certainly be outdated. A Parliamentary Select Committee was therefore set up in the summer of 1941 to look into the entire programme.

In the Committee's opinion the delay was owing to the Albemarle's unorthodox nature. In such judgement they were only partially correct, for it owed more to the decisions to separate the production team from the design team and establish an entirely new concern to manufacture the aircraft, and to the need to train a large workforce to build the aircraft components. For this the Ministries and not the Air Force, or the aircraft industry, were at fault. What the Committee were unable to pass judgement upon was the ultimate value of this new workforce. Years later it was to contribute with importance to other aircraft programmes, in particular those relating to the important Airspeed Horsa glider and of course the Mosquito. Rightly, the Committee pointed out that the decision to halt work on all but six production types in the summer of 1940 had brought an unfortunate slowing-up in new types of aircraft, had delayed the Albemarle, and that accidents had further retarded its progress. Major weight problems and the trouble with short-span wings had meant new jigging and brought many amendments to sub-contractors' plans.

It is probably true to say that to 1940—and in very many cases since—no aircraft-production organization had ever been presented at the outset of a new type with a complete and accurate set of working drawings with, for example, all bolt and rivet holes accurately positioned. This was certainly the case with the Albemarle. Many of the non-aircraft production units started making jigs and tools with much enthusiasm, to find only too often that the detail parts made from them would not fit together. Had an aircraft company, in particular the parent company familiar with the conventions and idiosyncrasies of its own design office, built the initial batches of components, these difficulties would have been sorted out as a matter of routine. Subsequent sub-contractors would then have been provided with accurate tooling information.

Modifications have always been the bane of aircraft-production engineers' lives, but they have learnt over many years how best to deal with them. Not so the initial sub-contractors of Albemarle components. Lack of experience in this field alone, coupled with a more than usual number of modifications arising from flight trials and other tests, and protracted indecision regarding operational roles, was probably as big a factor in delaying early production and inflating costs.

The Parliamentary Committee closely examined financial accounts relating to the aircraft. They discovered that £6 million had been spent before the Albemarle went into production, which was a great amount by the standards of those times.

Amazed at the cost they asked whether such a large sum had previously been spent in this manner and were told that the highest total ever had been £500,000, but that in that instance the engines, upon which another £300,000 had been invested, could easily be used for another type. Thus, £800,000 was the highest amount so far spent before the project referred to was abandoned. It is difficult to work out today's equivalent of that sum of £6 million but it might well be in excess of £80 million, which must be considered high. One can imagine the outcry in some quarters now at such expenditure—and the Albemarle was no TSR-2.

It was the opinion of the Committee that there had been a general desire for the Albemarle, with the Air Council, firms and many 'public men' advocating making use of material not likely to be in short supply in wartime. The amount of steel needed for the Albemarle was small; wood was easy to repair—but when it came to supplies of the latter it transpired that shipment from Canada was required, and that indigenous timber was insufficient in quantity and possibly quality. Those 'in the know' subsequently and erroneously pointed out that 'a wooden aircraft is not so fast and efficient as a metal machine' and that it could not carry an equivalent load, forgetting the de Havilland Comet racer and the Albatross airliner. The Air Ministry went on record as expressing the opinion that they never expected a first-class machine would evolve from composite construction, and that there would always be a weight penalty! A wooden mock-up was now said to have been a peacetime luxury, and at a time when the Air Ministry was ordering new types 'off the drawing board'. In the case of the Albemarle, they said, one of the greatest difficulties was that of the weight, which had been greatly underestimated by the design staff—as a result of which the wing area had to be much increased, with further weight problems.

As if that had not been enough there were problems with production. Armstrong Whitworth was busy with the Whitley and newer designs. The former was likely to remain in production at Coventry. Gloster Aircraft had no new type in view, although it was expected that they would build the first jet fighters. Space available after Gladiator production ceased could therefore be used for Albemarles. But Gloster's association with the Hawker Group meant that space at Hucclecote was given over to Hurricane production instead, after which the Typhoon would take its place.

As an alternative a new concern, A. W. Hawkesley Ltd., its name a contraction of the firms involved, was established on a site at Gloucester. It came into being on 1 April 1941. The new company took over part of the Gloster Aeroplane Co. works, also the Albemarle team—that part which could be spared—and then recruited such staff as it could find, under the control of Mr. Hugh Burroughes. He was presented with a mixed bag which was sorted out by the somewhat summary method of trial and error, but in time there was a marked improvement. In fact a team emerged which rapidly became successful and finally, when the roles for the Albemarles were established, had become first rate. There was, however, nothing that could be done to recover the costly delays between 1939 and 1941.

A financial statement for the programme as at 27 May 1941 showed that £5·6 million had been spent before any machine had been delivered for possible operational use, and that the current monthly expenditure, also in 1941 terms, was £300,000. The total estimated cost of the ordered airframes was likely to be £16 million, to which needed to be added £7 million to £10 million for engines and equipment giving a likely cost of over £25 million—well over £200 million in today's terms. This alarming state of affairs soon came to the notice of the ever-watchful Prime Minister. 'Had the contractors been kept to their original schedule of delivery,' he wrote, 'it can hardly be doubted that much money would have been saved, and the Air Force would have had at its disposal a number of aircraft it might have been able to use at maximum capacity.'

Among some members of the Select Committee there lurked the belief that the best thing now would be to cut the losses by abandoning the entire programme. How often have such notions been expressed where aircraft are concerned? At the very time that such ideas were being floated there were reports suggesting that, while the Albemarle was no glittering performer, it was better than had generally been expected.

Boscombe Down's estimates dated 12 August 1941 indicated that at a gross weight of 36,500 lb. the aircraft had a top speed of 260 m.p.h. at 14,000 ft., cruised at 202 m.p.h. T.A.S. at 15,000 ft. in M.S. gear and 220 m.p.h. T.A.S. at the same height in F.S. gear. Its economical cruising speed was 190–200 m.p.h. T.A.S. and the service ceiling 18,500 ft. It took about 1,200 yd. to clear 50 ft. on take off. With a 4,500 lb. load the range was 1,050 miles in still air, 1,700 miles with a 1,500 lb. load. Top T.A.S. speeds already recorded were 268 m.p.h. with P1360 at 13,200 ft., 247 m.p.h. for P1361 at 11,000 ft. and for P1362, 255 m.p.h. at 11,000 ft. at a weight of 33,500 lb. The last had an estimated absolute ceiling of 20,500 ft. although it had only been taken to 17,000 ft.

With these figures to hand, Lord Beaverbrook and Sir Archibald Sinclair, the Secretary of State for Air, decided on a middle-of-the-road course. On 19 September 1941 they proposed completion of only 500 of the aircraft on order.

The Prime Minister was uneasy about production delays, and the reasons for them, after reading the Select Committee's report. On 11 October 1941 he asked to know 'what real use the machine will be' when the first 500 were complete; whether it would be useful the following summer—and what part of Germany it could bomb, a typical Churchillian touch. Since the matter was to be debated in Parliament on the following Wednesday (without mentioning the aircraft type) he needed to be sure of his ground. Although there was uneasiness in the House over the whole affair, no decisive action was demanded. Then, as ever, there was lamentable lack of aviation expertise among the pontificating Members. Instead, the War Cabinet was to keep a watchful eye on the future of the programme, which was fully discussed by them on 6 January 1942. Two questions were posed—did the machine represent a good return for the labour and materials used, and should as many as 500 be built?

This meeting elicited that its production was divisible into three sections: (a) design and manufacture of components and the assembly of these; (b) final assembly; and (c) flight testing. Fabrication of materials for 500 Albemarles had been completed by August 1941 and components for 300 were in production. By the end of that month the expenditure of building 500 aircraft amounted to £7,685,000—£15,370 per airframe—and it was estimated that modifications to each would amount to £9,760—a total of £4,880,000—making the cost of each airframe minus engines, turrets and radio and much equipment, about £25,130 compared with £20,740 for each Whitley.

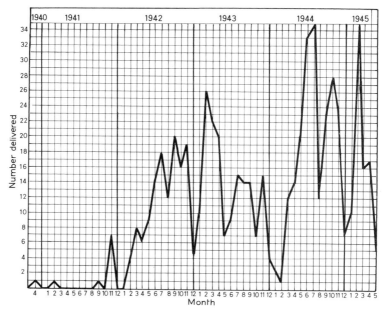

4. Delivery of Albemarles to the Royal Air Force—monthly totals

Cabinet conclusions were that even if manpower had been switched, or had been directed to the Whitley, this would have achieved little, since material for expanded Whitley production did not readily exist. Furthermore, if manpower was switched to any other project the wastage of materials collected for the Albemarle, and indeed the loss of 500 aircraft, would have been greater than anything incurred by carrying the aircraft through. So the Albemarle's future was now on fairly sound ground. The Select Committee considered that there had been lack of energy in pursuing the project, and wasteful expenditure. It did not, of course, pass anyone's notice that at one time the manufacturers had actually described it as 'a shoddy aircraft'. They meant, only, that component finish was poor but it was a very unfortunate statement to have made. The aircraft was, they said, better than the Anson—again, a curious statement for there were really no grounds at all for comparison.

'What shall we do with the Albemarle?'

While the Select Committee had been pondering the financial aspects of the Albemarle the Air Staff were grappling with a major question. By August 1941, before any production aircraft had been delivered, they had posed the question 'Once we have the Albemarle, what shall we do with it?' many times. Its production form offered no advance over the Wellington, and four-engined bombers were beginning to arrive in some numbers. In addition, when the question of the Albemarle's use was raised the Air Staff quickly pointed out that they had nothing to do with drawing up the requirement, and that the Director of Operational Requirements was being asked to draw up requirements to suit the machine. With production underway the Air Staff had now to decide how to employ the aeroplane.

As a front-line bomber it would clearly be a non-starter. One possibility was to use it for coastal reconnaissance, anti-submarine patrol and shallow convoy escort, for which there were needs at this time. But the Albemarle's effective range was about 400 miles less than the Wellington's, and its defensive armament was poor. The rejected ventral turret could, however, be replaced by an FN 64. Additions of ASV radar aerials would be essential for a general reconnaissance role, and this could only further reduce performance. The Albemarle's construction was quite unsuitable for the exposed and bad conditions that were so often encountered at Coastal Command stations. Replacement of the Hudson by the Albemarle could not, therefore, be recommended.

Another idea discussed was to use it in preference to the contentious Wellington for transport. After bombing gear and turrets were removed it looked likely to have a range of 1,400 miles and carry a load of about 6,500 lb. Because of its construction it appeared unsuitable for service in the Middle East, which was where such a machine was required. As a paratrooper it could, perhaps, carry sixteen men.

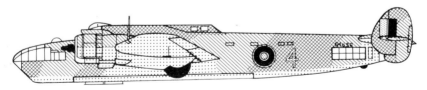

5. Albemarle Troop Carrier/Special Transport Mk. 1 P1650 exhibits the day bomber finish of some early Albemarles. This scheme was retained to the end of the war on examples not used for front-line airborne forces duty. P1650 went first to 39 M.U. on 24.2.43, to O.A.P.U. 19.4.43, 305 F.T.U. 26.4.43, 3 O.A.D.U., 2 O.A.P.U. and to the Air Transport Auxiliary on 3.3.44. It was struck off charge on 31.5.45, and is seen as recorded at Cambridge on 3.6.45 (For key to camouflage colours see page 100)

Could it replace the Wellington in bomber Operational Training Units? Not really, because its nosewheel undercarriage was almost unique among bombers at this stage. Another possible employment was as a glider tug, but doubts were expressed as to whether its airframe could withstand the stresses. Thus, it is hardly surprising to learn that, on 20 August 1941, the Director of Operational Requirements recorded that he could see no future for the Albemarle, and that the type was 'out of date before being launched'. He asked for an enquiry to see how much production could be reduced.

That the aircraft was already overweight was pointed out by the Vice-Chief of the Air Staff. He argued that if it carried ASV radar it would be unable to lift four depth charges and retain sufficient range. Owing to excessive weight, single-engined performance was very poor, but the Albemarle might be useful for the training of Liberator crews, and at a time when Liberators were to be extensively employed in No. 1 Group, Bomber Command. The turret arrangement, however, was quite different from that of all other R.A.F. bombers, which was disadvantageous for training purposes.

At the end of August 1941 the Albemarle's use for operational training was thoroughly examined. Belief then was that heavy bomber Operational Training Units would have to be formed, but that their numbers would still have to include 75 per cent medium bombers so that a Liberator O.T.U. would have only 25 per cent Liberators and 75 per cent mediums. But Liberator O.T.U.s—if formed— were to be sited in the U.S.A. It was decided to conduct trials with an Albemarle at an O.T.U. Using the aircraft as a gunnery or navigation trainer was also considered. As an aeroplane to replace the Whitley in air-gunnery schools the Albemarle offered no gunnery advantage, but it was decided to try an Albemarle at No. 2 Air Gunnery School, Millom. In addition, the Secretary of State for Air suggested its use as an air ambulance, and there were further suggestions for its use in air/sea rescue and night photography roles.

P1362, the third Albemarle, was delivered to A. & A.E.E. on 3 September 1941 and only three more were in Service hands by the close of 1941, which brought more misgivings about the whole scheme. Investigation of possibly gunnery-training use showed that the aeroplane's guns could not be depressed sufficiently for use against ground targets, and the use of a large aeroplane with only one turret was uneconomical. Possible rate of output of students, and its more sturdy construction, rendered the Avro Anson much better for observer training. Albemarles might be used to give advanced training for surplus aircrew for which about six squadrons could be formed in Bomber Command. Giving these each 24 I.E. aircraft with 30 per cent reserve would take up about 200 Albemarles, thus avoiding wastage of these aeroplanes. These six squadrons would be those that would later operate Liberators, but the Albemarles would remain non-operational trainers. Two Albemarle A.S.R. squadrons could also form, and glider towing might be a third employment, thus utilizing 500 aircraft.

On 4 October 1941 it was advocated that the first 200 Albemarles should be completed as fully-equipped medium bombers for the six squadrons, and that the remainder had best be fitted out as general purpose freighter/troop carriers

13. The first production Albemarle, P1362, wearing prototype markings and photographed in January 1942. The aircraft is wearing standard bomber camouflage

without bomb gear or turrets. This was agreed on 8 October as far as the first 200 were concerned. The next 200, it was decided, had better be completed in the light of experience with the first batch. In its air/sea rescue role the intention was that the Albemarle would carry an airborne lifeboat in its belly. But its single-engined performance was questionable—it probably would not fly on one engine above 29,500 lb. If some of the equipment were removed it might achieve a 600-mile range—1,150 miles on both engines, but only at 2,000 feet.

By October, trials had been undertaken with P1362 at A.& A.E.E. Its tare weight was 22,614 lb. (bomber), 22,614 lb. (reconnaissance), which gave 35,726 lb. and 36,439 lb. respectively at full load. The alternative weights were due to a fuel load of 769 gal. in the bomber and 1,399 gal. in the other role. Set against this the service load of the former was 7,039 lb. and 2,904 lb. in the reconnaissance aircraft. The latest trials showed a top speed, at loaded weight, of about 265 m.p.h. at 14,000 ft. and it cruised at 215 m.p.h. at 10,000 ft. Climb to 15,000 ft. took $28\frac{1}{2}$ minutes and the weak mixture take-off run was 1,080 yd., an improvement upon earlier tests. Range with maximum bomb load was now said to be 1,510 miles at 215 m.p.h., 1,820 miles at 170 m.p.h. at 10,000 ft.

Means were still being sought for disposal of the aircraft. One unkind notion was to sell it to Allied or friendly powers, and Brazil was mooted. But the D.O.R. considered it might still be useful as a transport or glider tug for which purposes Britain would always be short of aircraft. However, on 27 October 1941 it was confirmed that the first 200 would still be used for training Liberator crews, and serve at air-gunnery and bombing schools, but by mid-November another change was in vogue. Without any structural modifications the machine should be capable of conversion at short notice into a paratrooper. The hole left in the floor where the ventral turret had been sited was to be adapted to incorporate the lower portion of the paratroop cone, and the upper floor was to be modified. A circular hole 36 inches in diameter was thereby obtained which would be sealed by a fabric cover. As a pure freighter the Albemarle was still unappealing on account of its small payload.

Constant changes for future employment continued unabated and played havoc with factory work. Further suggestions that the whole scheme be cancelled were abandoned because it was now considered likely to be too disruptive. So, in early January 1942, after more deliberations, it was again decided that the first 200 aircraft—less a few to be used for night photography by P.R.U.—be built as medium bombers, and within a few days it had been decided to complete the remainder likewise. One aircraft was to go to the Middle East for climatic trials and assessment of its suitability as a freighter. What had brought about this change was the decision to form six fully-operational medium bomber Albemarle squadrons instead of the six 'shadow' squadrons formerly suggested. In mid-January 1942 the decision was made for production of the Albemarle Mk. II with up-rated Hercules VI engines, this to commence with the 201st machine.

Thirteen Albemarles were flying by the end of 1941 and it was believed that 100 would be flying by the end of June 1942. The first six examples were set aside for experimental flying. P1362 flew type trials at A. & A.E.E., P1363 was used at Baginton for general development, P1364 was retained at Hawkesley for trial installation work, P1365 went to A. & A.E.E. for intensive flying, P1368 was used at A. & A.E.E. for performance assessment and P1369 went to R.A.E. Farnborough for trial installation of photographic equipment for the P.R.U. Pending their introduction to service, production Albemarles had to remain in maintenance units, apart from P1376, delivered to the Torpedo Development Unit, Gosport, in April 1942 with a view to its being used for general reconnaissance development and as a trial installations aircraft. During early March 1942 a request had been received at Coventry for one aircraft to be adapted to carry torpedos in the belly, initially 18-inch torpedoes. Later, 22·4-inch torpedoes were specified. This was at a time when the Ministry of Aircraft Production was receiving urgent calls from Air Ministry to modify existing bomber types into possible torpedo carriers because torpedo bomber production was insufficient for needs. Because of the possibility of using the Albemarle as a makeshift torpedo bomber, despite its apparent unsuitability, the Air Ministry requested that a further 100 Albemarles be built, even before torpedo-dropping trials had been undertaken at T.D.U.

The Air Ministry was under the impression that orders had been given from the highest level to limit Albemarle production to 500 aircraft, but this was not so. Such an order was possible, however, because although the Gloster Meteor could still not be ready in time to follow the Albemarle, there was a chance that the Mosquito might follow it at Hawkesley. At this time the Air Staff considered the Albemarle could well become acceptable as a torpedo carrier, and if this became so then the additional order for 100 made sense.

Internal storage of Albemarles at maintenance units, for fear of weathering problems, was raising difficulties because of the space they occupied. Over fifty were in store by August 1942, when 41 Group requested that one be picked out to see how it would fare, for the aircraft would have to stand in the open at dispersals later.

Meanwhile Bomber Command had been assessing the suitability of the

Albemarle for operations. It seemed to the Commander-in-Chief that it was inferior in performance to the Wellington III now in use in numbers. Its defensive armament was too weak, particularly as a dustbin turret would have to be left extended to be of any use and that would reduce its speed by 20–25 m.p.h. and its range by 10 per cent. By now the general reconnaissance load capability consisted of 1,500 lb. of bombs for a range of 2,260 miles, and modifications permitted the carriage of two torpedoes or $2 \times 1,500$ lb. magnetic mines. As a bomber for operation over Germany it was quite unsuitable although it might have been of use overseas as a Wellington replacement, releasing later marks of that type for use in Bomber Command. On 16 August 1942, Sir Arthur Harris suggested that three Albemarles be sent to the Bomber Development Unit for full investigation of the type's bomber capabilities. This was at a time when Albemarles were being issued to a variety of units for trials. Three went to Army Co-operation Command for troop-carrier investigation, three to the Middle East for tropical trials and freighter suitability, one to the Central Gunnery School, four to meteorological flights, one to an A.S.R. unit and, as requested, three to B.D.U.

In September 1942, results of the tests at T.D.U. were to hand revealing the machine quite unsuited to the torpedo-bomber role. Its controls were too heavy, it lacked essential manoeuvrability, its take-off and landing runs were too long, the lateral view was poor, as was the turning circle; these all militated against its being used for torpedo attack. Apart from an acceptable layout, Coastal Command had no time for the aircraft, and were particularly against it for its poor single-engined performance. So, with Bomber and Coastal Command opting out of operating it, its future now lay mainly in a possible freighter/troop-carrying/glider-tug role.

By mid-1942 seventy-five Albemarles had been built. Twelve were now in service for trials, twenty-three were in M.U.s (without propellers fitted but could be made flyable at the rate of about seven per week) and another forty in 41 Group hands undergoing inspections in connection with possible wing-root problems. Details of the fleet as on 13 September 1942 are as follows:

At Armstrong Whitworth: P1363, P1376.
At Hawkesley for development: P1364.
At A. & A.E.E.: P1369, P1362, P1437.
At Netheravon with Army Co-operation Command: P1430, P1436, P1438.
At R.A.E.: P1394.
At Filton being prepared for tropical trials: P1449, P1371, P1370, P1453.
At Airborne Forces Experimental Establishment: P1402, P1366.
At Central Gunnery School: P1439.
With Meteorological Flights: P1373 (521 Squadron), P1442 (1404 Met. Flt.), P1408 (1406 Met. Flt.).
At B.D.U.: P1459, P1460, P1461.
With Coastal Command: P1409 (279 Squadron), P1431 (Coastal Command Development Unit, Tain).
With 271 Transport Squadron: P1405, P1407.
At Marshall's Flying School, Cambridge, for modifications and trial overhaul by

14. Some Albemarle bombers were finished in day bomber camouflage which also suited them for possible service with Coastal Command. P1372 shown here is wearing Dark Green and Dark Earth upper surfaces and Sky undersurfaces. After A. & A.E.E. trials P1372 was modified for 511 Squadron and later served with 42 O.T.U.

the appointed Civilian Repair Organization: P1365, P1372 and P1375.

Proposals at this time were that about thirty Albemarles be allocated for use in meteorological flights, eighty for A.S.R. use, twenty C.G.S. and about forty for Bomber Command O.T.U.s. If transport trials were successful forty to fifty would be set aside for that role. These were times of flux where employment was concerned, and it can be seen how difficult it was for the Air Staff to find a niche for the aircraft.

Supply of Hercules engines in the summer of 1942 was critical. It had been the intention that some Short Stirling bombers would be fitted with American engines, but they conferred little advantage to that aircraft. Therefore it was now suggested that the fitting of American engines in the Albemarle could release much-needed Hercules engines. It was computed that such an Albemarle could carry 5,000 lb. of freight for a practical range of 1,270 miles once bombing gear was deleted. Armstrong Whitworth had looked into this possibility two years previously, and had given some assistance to Short Bros. when they were wedding American engines to the Stirling. In September 1942 the order was given for a prototype conversion to be produced using P1406. This was fitted with two

15. Albemarle Mk. IV P1406 fitted with Double Cyclone engines, and photographed at Boscombe Down in February 1943. Completed in May 1942, it was struck off charge in August 1945

Wright Cyclone GR-2600 A5Bs. Tare weight worked out to be 22,889 lb., fuel 769 gal., oil 59 gal. and loaded weight 36,026 lb. The c.g. was 76·9 in. aft when loaded compared with 75·8 in. in the normal bomber and 78·8 in. in the G.R. Hercules version. The performance differed little, and later a second prototype was built for further trials, before events overtook the machine. This variant came into play at a time when the suggestion had arisen of passing Albemarles to the Russians. To release much-wanted Hercules engines made no sense, hence the value of a possible Cyclone version.

Results of the trials being undertaken by various organizations were coming to hand by the end of October 1942. Again, the machine was declared unsuitable for gunnery training. For meteorological reconnaissance on *Rhombus* flights it would need to fly in very poor weather and bad visibility. Limited pilot's view made the Albemarle unsuitable for such employment, and it had no de-icing gear. For A.S.R. work a good field of view was needed. If an Albemarle pilot sighted a dinghy he would have difficulty in maintaining contact, it was argued. The aircraft's defensive capability was also judged poor for this role. So, if the Albemarle was to be of any use, it must now be as a transport/glider tug. It could carry twenty passengers seated facing inwards on small seats mounted on movable beams bolted to the floor and similar in fit to aircraft which it was soon decided to release to the U.S.S.R. In October 1942 the order to proceed was given for seventy-one aircraft to be modified into transports, with tests to follow. Five fits were listed, as follows: (a) With or without long-range tanks.

(b) With or without long-range tanks in a passenger-cum-freight version.

(c) No long-range tanks in a fit for paratrooping/supply-dropping role.

(d) Glider tug without long-range tanks.

(e) Stretcher-carrying with or without long-range tanks.

It was at the end of 1942 that the Soviet Ambassador asked the British Government whether they could supply any transport aircraft, after earlier contact on this point. The British had replied that they had none to spare but, realizing there would be surplus Albemarles, now suggested that the Russians might find a use for this aircraft. Russian officials inspected the Albemarle at Cambridge and seeing its potential (and doubtless knowing little of its unhappy history) took an immediate liking to it. There can be no denying that it was an appealing-looking aeroplane, and if one acquiesces to the view that aeroplanes 'which look right are right', then one would have expected all to be well with the Albemarle. The British Government, happy to rid themselves of their creation, offered to supply the Russians with 100 Albemarles by the end of March 1943, and in the meantime the Russians asked for a further 100. At this period, it will be recalled, the aircraft was still earmarked for bomber-crew training. If it did not fill that role then Wellingtons would have to be diverted from other duties, so there was hesitancy about granting the Russian request.

Now a new problem was pressing. The airborne forces squadrons were employing Whitleys as operational paratroopers and glider tugs, indeed using them for bombing raids and leaflet drops on French targets. Whitleys were outdated and it was soon obvious that the only aeroplane to hand which could possibly replace the Whitley was the Albemarle—always assuming that it could tow a loaded Airspeed Horsa glider. The airborne forces desired a new tug and the quick decision was made that led to an order to proceed with Albemarles for the task.

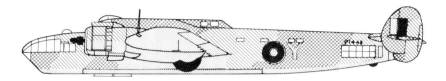

6.   Albemarle S.T.Mk. 1 P1448. initially delivered to 6 M.U. 30.7.42, to 39 M.U. 25. 9.42, to 2 O.A.P.U. 7.1.43, 205 F.T.U. 4.1.44, 2 O.A.P.U. 20.4.44 and to the O.R.T.U. Hampstead Norris 2.5.44. It was struck off charge there on 27.1.45 and promptly flown to Cambridge to be reduced to produce. It is depicted as seen on 4.2.45. Cargo doors had been fitted to the starboard side of the rear fuselage, and Type C roundels were to be seen above the wing tips. The Dark Green–Dark Earth–Azure Blue finish was common on Albemarle Special Transports serving in Britain as well as overseas (For key to camouflage colours see page 100)

Development was now concentrated on its use in a transport role and any commitment to bombing and reconnaissance in any form was now dropped. Two boat-like panniers were to fit into the bomb cell and extend well below the line of the fuselage, rather in the manner of the freight compartment of the Warwick Freighter. These panniers would be winched up and into the cell then locked into position using bolts. All armament would be removed from such aircraft. These modifications were soon deemed far too extensive to adopt so, instead, the machines selected for the Special Transport role merely had turrets and bomb gear removed and seats fitted as needed. The idea of belly panniers was dropped and freight, if carried, would have to be loaded inside the fuselage. One trial aircraft flew with a special pannier beneath each outer wing panel and this could contain up to four paratroops, but such an alarming scheme was soon abandoned. For paratroop-dropping the fuselage ventral exit was enlarged. In such Albemarles, sub-designated 'Troop Carrier', the bomb-release system and racks were retained for supply containers. Thus, bombs could still be dropped.

The Albemarle in service

At the close of November 1942 two Albemarles on the strength of Ferry Units were detached to No. 511 Squadron at Lyneham, Wiltshire. At 23.45 hours on 1 December P1453 took off, carrying 3,000 lb. of freight for a night journey to Gibraltar where it touched down at 08.25 hours, thereby completing the first operational flight by the type, nearly five years and countless discussions after it had been conceived. P1499 made the next trials flight, on 6 December, lifting 2,966 lb. of freight and mail on a similar night sortie which took it some way out over the Atlantic. A third Gibraltar flight was flown on 15 January, again by P1453.

16.   Albemarle 1 P1514 was modified to a Transport (Lyneham Standard) and then joined 511 Squadron in June 1943 for six months' service. Its finish is Dark Green and Dark Earth with Azure Blue undersurfaces

In February the first allocation of Albemarles specially modified for the Lyneham–Gibraltar–Algiers route was made, these aircraft being designated Mk. I (Transport Command, Lyneham Standard). Loads of up to 5,000 lb. could be transported in the fuselage of the Albemarle (Russian Transport Type), or 4,000 lb. in the centre of the fuselage of the bomber type. These special Lyneham conversions had their dorsal turrets removed and their undersurfaces repainted Azure Blue to suit them for flights to the Middle East. P1564 was, on 18 February 1943, the first Albemarle to be allocated to No. 511 Squadron and within the next few days P1475, P1510, P1520, P1556 and P1561 joined the squadron.

By February 1943, 104 standard Mk. I bombers had been built of which sixty-one remained in 41 Group and seventy-three had been converted to Russian Transport standard, with a large cargo door in the rear fuselage. Turrets had been removed. The current plan was to produce 200 such aircraft. On 11 February after discussions with 38 Wing it was decided that some Albemarles would be fitted to tow Horsas, so at last the Albemarle had found some use.

From now onwards the fortunes of the Albemarle were closely tied to those of 38 Wing (later 38 Group) and the airborne forces. By mid-1942 the Wing had two Whitley squadrons up to strength, 296 Squadron specializing in paratroop delivery and No. 297 in glider towing. There was a shortage of operational gliders and sixty or so Whitleys in hand were deemed useless for operational glider-tug duty. As early as June 1942 the Albemarle had been offered to 38 Wing, but they had been hesitant to accept it. Now it was the only foreseeable aeroplane that could replace the Whitley. It could carry up to fifteen paratroops, although ten men and their equipment were a more realistic load. This was an improvement upon the Whitley, and the Albemarle was faster. Its nosewheel undercarriage made it easier to tow off a glider, but A.F.E.E. tested an Albemarle and insisted that it could not maintain over 700 feet with a fully loaded Horsa in tow. At 38 Wing H.Q. the Staff found this hard to accept and further trials at

Netheravon showed the machine far more successful if the fuel load was reduced. This would be an acceptable limitation during operations against close Continental dropping zones. On 30 January 1943, P1446 reached 296 Squadron at Hurn, the first machine to join an airborne squadron. Strength was then slowly built up.

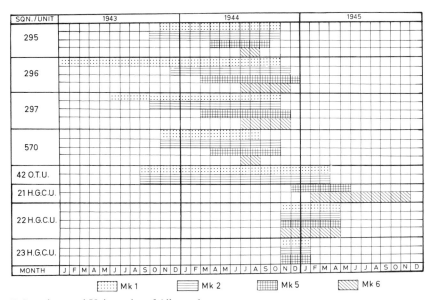

7. Squadron and Unit service of Albemarles

Satisfaction set the airborne forces requesting more Albemarles and led to a drastic reduction in the number made available to the Russians who ultimately received only thirteen: five in March 1943 and eight—one of which was lost *en route*—in April 1943. What use the U.S.S.R. made of them has never been established. Delivery to Russia prompted the modification of four Mk. Is designated Mk. I (Special Ferrying) for the use of British ferry pilots who delivered the aircraft to Russia.

At Hurn 296 Squadron worked up fast on the new type, and on the night of 9/10 February 1943, P1446 (Wg. Cdr. P. R. May) and P1521 (Sqn. Ldr. P. B. N. Davies) made the first venture across the Channel, the first dropping leaflets on Rouen and the second having to abort before reaching the target at Lisieux. On 11 February Davies dropped leaflets on Paris from P1521.

For the Albemarles 19 February 1943 was a special night. This was one of only two occasions when they were called upon to drop bombs in anger. P1446, P1462, P1466 and P1521 set off, in company with five Whitleys, for a raid on Creny in France. But the Albemarles, never in luck, found the night dark and the weather very poor, so much so that the entire force had to abandon the operation. The only other bombing raid was mounted on 17 April. Seven Albemarles (P1380,

17. One of the batch of Albemarles passed to the U.S.S.R. A large cargo door has been fitted to the starboard rear side of the fuselage, and the Red Star insignia appears on the fuselage and upon both sides of the fins. The dorsal turret has been replaced by the standard two-gun mounting as fitted to Special Transport variants of the Albemarle

P1528, P1430, P1442, P1515, P1521 and P1446) were despatched mostly to Conde-sur-Huisme. Of the force Sqn. Ldr. P. B. N. Davies bombed Letheil and Sgt. L. Brydon bombed Melden rail junction. This was the final operation by 296 Squadron over France at this time. In all, seventeen Albemarle sorties had been flown, all at night.

No. 38 Wing was warned in March 1943 that they might soon have to despatch some of their Albemarles to North Africa. As soon as the North Africa coastal region was in Allied hands airborne forces would take part in an attack on southern Europe in conjunction with American airborne forces. An advanced party in P1382, flown by Flg. Off. Cumberworth left on 23 May as the first movement of the Main Party in Operation *Beggar*, which began on 3 June, Flg. Off. V. G. Houchin (P1443) and Sqn. Ldr. L. C. Bartram (P1552) leaving on the long flight to Froha, Algeria, via Gibraltar, to form the squadron's main advanced party.

Thirty-three flights had been made by 10 June without loss. In addition to passengers and freight, the aircraft carried about 1,190 gallons of fuel, and set off loaded at around 36,500 lb. They were despatched by No. 3 Overseas Air Delivery Unit, Hurn, and ordered to land at Gibraltar if the weather was uncertain or fuel was short, or if they had mechanical trouble. Some managed the direct flight to Froha, a 10- to 12-hour journey flown by single pilots. The Albemarles which made the flight were: P1448, P1469, P1375, P1444, P1440, P1501, P1453, P1517, P1551, P1434, P1518, P1525, P1467, P1470, P1466, P1522, P1437, P1516, P1446, P1512, P1553, P1432, P1526, P1527, P1474, P1439, P1557, P1527, P1443, P1552, P1389, P1528 and P1382.

Behind the move was a three-fold plan. On the first night of the offensive a glider-borne force would seize a bridgehead near Syracuse in Sicily. Next night more gliders would land near Augusta twenty miles away. On the following night a third landing was planned, to take place near Catania. A Halifax squadron and elements of the U.S.A.A.F. would also take part in the assaults. Before the operation could be mounted many exercises had to be flown, and there was still much to do by way of operational trials. Some Albemarles would tow Horsas, others American Waco CG-4A Hadrian gliders, the first CG-4A tow being attempted by Sqn. Ldr. Davies on 9 June. A daylight paratroop drop was made on 12 June, each Albemarle carrying nine fully armed men. On 20 June twenty-two Albemarles managed to get airborne, each towing a Hadrian. Glider towing made the engines run at high temperatures and so modifications had to be made to the oil coolers, but this resulted in only a 5 per cent reduction. Fuel consumption with a loaded glider in tow worked out at about 160 gallons per hour.

Next came the move to the operational airfield, Goubrine II, near Sidi-el-Ma not far from Kairouan in Tunisia. To reach it, the Albemarles, each with a glider in tow, began on 24 June to make the 5-hour flight over 530 miles of mountainous terrain. Initially it had been the intention that Halifaxes of 295 Squadron would tow Horsas to Sicily and the Albemarles take the paratroops there, but insufficient Halifaxes and crews had brought about changes in the plan. The big question now was—could the Albemarle successfully tow a loaded glider in a warm climate? On 3 July Sqn. Ldr. Davies had a try and later flew a fuel-consumption test over the sea. The Albemarle towed the Horsa off, but the engine temperatures ran to 100° F. It was possible, although there would be scarcely sufficient fuel left to make the return flight from Sicily. Training and trials did not proceed without incident. Flg. Off. F. L. Hopkinson made a landing approach but had to go round again and in so doing stalled, hitting P1552 on dispersal. His aircraft, P1522, crashed and was destroyed.

This accident came upon the very day that the first stage of the operation was to take place, 9 July. At 19.25 hours the first Albemarle, P1446, flown by the squadron commander, Wg. Cdr. P. R. May, took off, towing a Horsa. It is believed to have been the first to release its glider over Sicily. The other twenty-four Albemarles all towed Waco CG-4As. P1373, P1518, P1521, P1434, P1382, P1389, P1466, P1469, P1467, P1437, P1470, P1557, P1501, P1517, P1525 all towed their gliders safely to the island, but P1516, P1526, P1553 and P1444 cast theirs off only for them to fall into the sea off Syracuse. The gliders behind P1453, P1551 and P1440 cast off too soon after take off and the tugs made early returns. P1474 and P1437 aborted, the latter due to engine trouble. Seventeen crews claimed that their gliders were released within the Landing Zone, and all of the tugs returned safely from Operation *Ladbroke*. It was impossible to mount another glider drop the following night, for the weather did not permit it. On the night of 12/13 July two Albemarles were despatched, P1446 (Wg. Cdr. May) and P1526 (Flt. Lt. Smulley), each carrying ten Special Air Service saboteurs to attack behind enemy lines in Operation *Chestnut 1*. Between Malta and Catania both aircraft encountered anti-aircraft fire from Allied shipping and it was believed that it was this that shot down P1446 whose crew was posted missing.

On 13/14 July the second phase of the main operation went forward, with the execution of Operation *Fustian*. Its purpose was to take paratroops and gliders with troops and equipment to the Primosole Bridge leading from the hills into the Catania region, and to hold that bridge until it was reached by troops of the 8th Army advancing along the east coast of Sicily. Ten Albemarles took off, each with ten troops of the 1st Parachute Brigade and their Head Quarters. These aircraft were: P1518, P1526, P1432, P1389, P1512, P1453, P1516, P1434, P1382 and P1525. The drop was to be on the Catania Plain where P1468 was to drop ten S.A.S. troops. Next came a dozen Albemarles towing gliders—P1501, P1437, P1551, P1521 (flown by Flt. Lt. V. Houchin and lost in action) and P1517 all towing Hadrians. P1466 also towing a Hadrian, and flown by Plt. Off. G. R. Wilson, crashed on take off. P1474, also with a Hadrian, lost its glider and turned back. P1469 was the only aircraft whose glider landed north of the river although its troops were later joined by those from a Horsa. Four Albemarles towed Horsas, P1467, P1553, P1440, and P1444 which, flown by Flg. Off. R. T. Haymer, did not return. Two others carried S.A.S. troops but, on receiving no signal from the Dropping Zone, P1373 did not drop its load. The ten men were brought back. P1437 was hit by flak when turning out to sea after its drop. Control surfaces were damaged and the aircraft was ditched, the crew being picked up by a destroyer. Flak, particularly from Allied ships, damaged a number of aircraft. For eighteen hours the Primosole Bridge was held, lost then recaptured. On 14 July, P1474 and P1525 each took ten S.A.S. troops to Sicily for saboteur operations. *Fustian* had hardly been a success, but this was not attributable to the performance of the aircraft. Less than half the gliders landed on the island and only sixteen anywhere near the Landing Ground. Casualties among troops were high, too.

Following the operation, 296 Squadron was held ready for possible operations against the mainland of Italy. Unreinforced Whitley tyres had been fitted to the Albemarles and they were wearing badly at their sides. Brakes were overheating too. The aircraft were grounded, the main source of trouble being the heavy loads imposed upon them when flying with gliders. Spares became an increasing problem and to conserve engines flying was cut to a minimum. During August and September sixteen more Albemarles (P1401, P1384, P1464, P1461, P1383, P1342, P1365, P1471, P1430, P1391, P1367, P1396, P1394, P1364, P1511 and one other) arrived from Britain to keep the unit up to strength. This was necessary since, by the end of July, only five Albemarles remained serviceable and fifteen were grounded by lack of tyres. P1440 had crashed on take off from Goubrine on 22 July and P1474 crashed on landing on 31 July. By mid-August only two of the original aircraft were serviceable. However, a detachment of the squadron moved to Cassabile in Sicily on 29 August from where, on 30 August, dummy paratroops were dropped on the toe of Italy. S.A.S. troops were also dropped before the detachment ended on 12 September. A further detachment was made, to Torrento Communeldi, between 9 and 13 October. On 7 September P1551 and P1525 flew S.A.S. troops to Northern Italy and it is believed that these two aircraft were the last R.A.F. machines to operate over that country before the Italian Government capitulated.

Delivery of mail commenced on 15 September, to Grottaglie, near Taranto, and continued into October. On 2 October the last drop from No. 2 S.A.S. Regiment was made, to a point seven miles west of Chieti, by P1434, P1435, P1467 and P1469. The Albemarle's possible use, now that Italy had capitulated, was limited and so between 15 and 25 October 26 Albemarles were flown home to Hurn, aircraft P1432, P1373, P1430, P1467, P1392, P1550, P1391, P1512, P1461, P1434, P1435, P1557, P1471, P1511, P1464, P1501, P1551, P1384, P1396, P1469, P1394, P1387, P1409, P1367, P1380, P1518. Fifteen Albemarles had been lost in the campaign, during operations or as a result of accidents. From now onwards the scene of Albemarle operations would be north-west Europe.

The planned strength of 38 Group, formed out of 38 Wing, was four squadrons of Stirling IVs, two of Halifaxes and four of Albemarles. It was to be supported by five Dakota squadrons in 46 Group, the whole force to be large enough to move an airborne division. Its purpose was to provide transport for the opening assault when the Allies decided to land upon the mainland of Europe.

Already the second Albemarle trooping squadron had been equipped, No. 297 based at Thruxton, which took on charge P1399—its first machine—on 1 July 1943, P1401 on 14 July and P1384, P1387 and P1388 on 16 July. It commenced leaflet-dropping over France on 16 August 1943 using P1384, P1478, P1464 and P1405. On 1 September the squadron moved to Stoney Cross, coming off operations to train for the primary role. Halifaxes were still in short supply and since the intended theatre of operations was satisfied by short-range Albemarles these began to replace the Halifaxes in No. 295 Squadron with the arrival of V1647 on 14 October, as a result of which the squadron's Halifaxes passed to 298 Squadron. Within the next few days V1602, V1608, V1613 and V1626 arrived. These aircraft were all Albemarle IIs and aircraft of this mark with Hercules VI engines were also introduced to No. 297 Squadron at this time.

In November 1943 the American-engined Albemarle IV was finally dropped after two examples had been produced for trials. It was further decided that all future Albemarles would equate Mk. II standard, but that from the 397th airframe a large freight door would be incorporated into the aft port side of the fuselage. Such aircraft were designated Mk. VI, but earlier machines were also modified to have the cargo door.

Retrospective designations had now been issued for the Albemarle. The Mk. I series i was the original version produced as a bomber-reconnaissance aircraft. Some of these were modified into Mk. I srs. ii when Malcolm glider-towing gear was fitted along with a wire frame at the rear of the fuselage to prevent parachute fouling of the rear of the aircraft. These aircraft became generally known as G.T. Mk. I. A third variant in use was the S.T.I. (i.e. Special Transport Mk. I), a revision of the srs. i for 511 Squadron at Lyneham. Bombing gear was removed, the rear fuselage tank too. A hand-operated two-gun installation covered by a sliding hood replaced the dorsal turret. These special aircraft had a freight-loading door in the rear fuselage. Whereas the glider tugs and paratroopers were finished in Dark Green–Dark Earth–Night (black) camouflage like normal bombers (the upper surfaces replaced by two tones of brown on aircraft used in

18.   Many of the late production Albemarles served with training units, or never passed beyond Maintenance Units. V1875 depicted here, a Mk. VI, photographed in July 1944, was used by Nos. 23 and 21 H.G.C.U.s

North Africa in 1943) the S.T.I.s had either Sky or Azure Blue undersurfaces, the upper camouflage colours extending to the base of the fuselage and over the fins and rudders. Some of the Special Transports, the srs. ii, had provision for glider towing. Prior to this there had been other sub-designations for the aircraft—'38 Group Standard Troop Carrier G.T. Mk. I' for a batch beginning P1402 as well as 'Transport Standard Lyneham Standard' for those which 511 Squadron initially operated.

Many Mk. Is were returned to Hawkesley from M.U.s and squadrons for modifications for transport roles, and from June 1942 Marshall's Flying School at Cambridge became the Civilian Repair Organization responsible for major repairs and overhauls of the Albemarles, a task retained until the war ended. Many Albemarles were brought to these works after being struck off charge, their remains being 'cannibalized'.

Delivery of the last Mk. I to the R.A.F. came on 19 March 1943. Production of the Mk. II commenced with Troop Carrier (38 Group Standard) machines, commonly called G.T. Mk. II, from V1606 delivered 3 April 1943, and most were known as G.T. Mk. IIa. V1599, the first Mk. II, flew in February 1943 and the first delivered from the works was V1598 on 7 March 1943. The Mk. III Albemarle was a projected version powered by Rolls-Royce Merlin engines, but there were better uses for the Merlin and this version was not proceeded with. The Mk. IV has already been referred to. P1406, the American-engined Mk. IV, appeared mid-1942 and spent most of that year at A. & A.E.E. A second example of the Mk. IV appeared later as V1760 and was despatched to A. & A.E.E. on 16 August. This machine had a rear freight door like the Mk. VI.

The Mk. V incorporated various modifications including fuel jettisoning gear. The Mk. VI srs. i was similar to the Mk. V apart from the freight door, whereas the Mk. VI srs. ii had its turret replaced by a fairing similar to that of the earlier Special Transports. The first Mk. V, V1761 appeared early in 1944. V1766 was, on 17 March, the first to be delivered to the R.A.F. The first Mk. VI was delivered on 6 June 1944.

Expansion of 38 Group demanded more crews for the Albemarle squadrons. Accordingly, in September 1943, Whitleys of No. 42 O.T.U., Ashbourne, began to be replaced by Albemarle Is and IIs. Supply permitted the equipment of the fourth Albemarle squadron, No. 570, formed at Hurn on 15 November 1943 and equipped with sixteen I.E. and four I.R. aircraft. Personnel came from Nos. 295 and 296 Squadrons, and the final squadron was put under the command of Wg. Cdr. R. M. Bangay. On 19 November 1943 six Albemarles arrived on loan from 295 Squadron and on 26th 570 Squadron took on charge two Mk. IIs from Hawkesley. No. 570 Squadron was equipped with Mk. IIs apart from three Mk. Is. By the end of 1943 equipment of the four planned squadrons was complete.

Many glider-towing exercises were flown as the retrieval of Horsas from dispersal airfields had to be undertaken in early 1944, and to have congregated the gliders at a few sites would have made them ideal incendiary targets on account of their wooden construction. By March 1944 the Horsas were nearly all at their operational bases and the Albemarle force was now freed for small-scale night operations in support of the French Underground movement. On 3 February the four squadrons commenced the operations which were to take place over the next three months. These activities were a sideline to the main job in hand, intensive working-up for the invasion of France. Many exercises—by day and night—with paratroops and gliders, were held in south, central and eastern England for the great assault planned. And so to June 1944.

8. Albemarle Glider Tug/Troop Carrier Mk. 1 P1399 was delivered to 44 M.U. on 16.6.42, to Hawkesley 30.5.43 and joined 297 Squadron on 1.7.43. After more than a year with the squadron it arrived at Cambridge on 7.8.44 on which date its markings shown here were recorded. It left for 5 M.U. in mid-December 1944 and was struck off charge on 26.11.45. As was standard on Albemarles with night finish, the fuselage serials were Dull Red (For key to camouflage colours see page 100)

19. The wing setting of the Albemarle gave it the appearance of a shoulder wing layout, evident on this Mk. V

Air tests on the morning of 5 June were followed in the afternoon by final briefings for Operation *Tonga* which was, at last, to take place on the night of 5/6 June 1944. This was to prove the highlight of the Albemarle's career. At Harwell and Brize Norton the Albemarles were marshalled into positions so that, if needed, gliders could be quickly attached to the tow ropes or paratroops emplaned.

Three phases marked the role of the Albemarle squadrons. Firstly, a small number were to set off ahead of the Main Force to drop paratroopers, some acting as 'pathfinders' for the Main Force who were to set up radio beacons to lead other aircraft to their correct destination zones. Others would also make a rapid attempt to hold small, yet vital, objectives in Normandy. Thus, the Albemarles would spearhead the whole assault. Secondly, there would come the Main Force of paratroopers and, thirdly, Albemarles towing Horsas. The Albemarle force totalled ninety-three aircraft, four of which came from 42 O.T.U. and operated from Hampstead Norris. The standard paratroop load of ten men was to be taken, and in their bomb bays the aircraft took along supplies.

Six Albemarles took off from Harwell one hour before midnight, V1740, V1656 and V1764 of 295 Squadron with V1814, V1695 and V1617 of 570 Squadron. These carried the 'pathfinders': two Albemarles dropping twenty troops at each of the three D.Z.s. On D.Z. 'L' only one aircraft dropped accurately, on D.Z. 'N' three sticks fell but were not correctly positioned. On D.Z. 'V' although the drop was accurate the beacons set up for reinforcements would not work. Consequently, when the Main Force arrived it was inevitably scattered, although the paratroops soon sorted themselves out for operations. Thirty-five more Albemarles then delivered paratroopers, most taking ten, and a few nine, troops. Drawn from the four squadrons the aircraft used were: 295 Squadron—V1753, P1430, V1784, V1751; 296 Squadron—V1701, V1765, V1774, V1699, V1696, V1616, V1605, V1744, V1630, V1698, V1501; 297 Squadron—P1384, P1383, V1716, P1400, V1700, V1812, P1365, V1743, P1367, V1772, V1742, P1471, P1378; 570 Squadron–V1645, V1704, V1653, P1379, V1627,

V1842, P1441, and from 42 O.T.U. P1442 (missing) and three others. V1605 also failed to return.

The main assault then followed, forty-five Albemarles each towing a Horsa. Five gliders prematurely cast off, and others were taken into battle to replace them. The Albemarles used were: 295 Squadron—V1757, V1647 (glider aborted), V1750, V1777, P1436 (glider aborted), V1766, P1369, V1607, V1763, V1748, P1445, P1397 with troops aboard, P1404, V1613, V1723 and V1749 the latter carrying General Gale and Divisional H.Q.; 296 Squadron—V1785, V1646, V1810, V1632, V1813, V1739, V1775, V1439; 297 Squadron—V 1781, V1823, V1778 (glider aborted), V1825, P1395, P1651, P1409, V1771, V1769; 570 Squadron—V1620 (glider aborted), V1746 (glider aborted), V1613, V1623, V1752, V1626, V1767, V1624, V1754, V1703, V1602 and P1380. All returned safely.

With the night's work complete the crews rested during the day, then in the afternoon, while ground crews remarshalled the aircraft alongside their runways, briefing took place for a second operation. The strength of 38 and 46 Groups was insufficient to permit them to take the entire British airborne force in one lift and so Operation *Mallard* was set for the evening of 6 June. Being a daylight operation it was heavily escorted by fighters. Each of the Albemarles involved towed a Horsa and were: 295 Squadron—V1656, V1780, V1753, P1404, V1766, V1764, V1751, V1613, V1809, V1723, V1820 (glider aborted), P1396, P1430, V1819, V1601, V1787, P1436, V1777; 296 Squadron—V1774, V1616, V1605, V1821, V1818, V1701, V1699, V1696, V1785, V1501, V1810, V1815, P1388, P1387, V1646, P1394, P1391, V1630; 297 Squadron—V1781, V1778, V1823, V1776, P1395 (glider aborted), P1460, P1409, P1378, P1471, V1773 (missing), V1825, V1772, V1769, V1782, V1841, V1716, V1372 and one other; 570 Squadron—V1645, V1627, V1756, V1620, V1642, P1557, V1653, V1643, V1704, V1814, V1761, V1617, V1811, V1816, V1842, P1441, V1783, V1694, P1371 and V1746. Once these major lifts were completed the crews stood by in case further operations were needed, but none was called for. Some small-scale drops followed and on 7/8 June crews of the four squadrons flew a small-scale operation, code-named *Cooney*, which consisted of lifting French paratroopers to the beachhead area to join French Underground fighters and attack bridges and other vulnerable points behind the lines.

Supply drops to the French Underground were then resumed, extending to early September. It was then time to prepare for the next major airlift, Operation *Market*. By now, however, supplies of Stirling IVs and Halifaxes were sufficient for the Albemarle squadrons to be cut by half. On 28 July Flg. Off. P. V. Wood flying P1461 made 295 Squadron's final Albemarle sortie, dropping supplies to the Maquis. No. 570 Squadron flew its last operational Albemarle sortie on 25 July, by which time both squadrons were equipping with Stirlings. No. 511 Squadron, which had been using Special Transports on the UK–Gibraltar–North Africa route since December 1942, had relinquished services with the aircraft in March 1944.

Operation *Market*, the Arnhem landing, took place to enable important

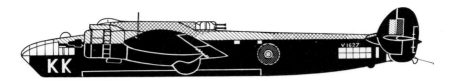

9. Albemarle G.T.IIa V1627 went initially to 38 M.U. on 25.8.43 and after overhaul and modification joined 570 Squadron on 2.12.43. It was flown to Cambridge for repair on 6.1.44, but instead was struck off charge on 7.2.44. It is depicted in the late 1943 markings of 570 Squadron prior to the introduction of squadron code letters (For key to camouflage colours see page 100)

bridges across the Rhine to be captured and held long enough for the main British and Canadian Army Groups to reach them and cross the river, preparatory for a rapid thrust along the northern coast of Holland into Germany. Unbeknown to the Allies strong German forces existed in the Arnhem area, and the airborne troops were insufficient in strength to capture and hold their objectives. For their part in the operation the two Albemarle squadrons moved forward to Manston where the huge runway, built to accommodate crippled aircraft, was ideal for marshalling and take off of gliders and tugs, for each machine would tow a Horsa on two operations. Final briefing for the crews of both squadrons took place at 08.00 hours on 17 September 1944. At mid-morning they went out to their aircraft, 296's spreading for 300 yards along one side of the landing strip which left 2,000 yards clear for take off. The runway was luckily set into wind and at 10.20 hours the first combination was away. Every aircraft was serviceable and fifty-five Albemarles towing Horsas took off within 45 minutes. There was a short pause, then the remaining five each towed off a Waco Hadrian. The large force assembled over south-east England, set course for the North Foreland and—over the North Sea—the Albemarles took their places in the majestic stream. Ahead were the Dakotas of 46 Group and to the rear was the armada of Stirlings and Halifaxes. As they approached the Dutch coast swarms of Allied fighters wheeled above and below, some dealing with a few flak outposts cheeky enough to interfere. The journey to the Landing Zone took the force for seventy miles over Holland before release was made from 2,000 feet. Once the gliders had been cast off the tugs flew on to drop their tow ropes then beat it fast at 6,000 feet for Manston where the Albemarles were speedily remarshalled for the next day's operation. One aircraft of 296 Squadron had been grazed by flak. Among those who had taken part was Wg. Cdr. Musgrave who had lost a leg on a glider accident in August 1943 and on this day flew an Albemarle which towed a Hadrian. The Albemarles which had taken part were: 296 Squadron—V1646, V1866, V1818, V1632, V1785, V1813, P1387, P1432, P1435, V1844, V1847, V1775, V1698, V1752, V1871, V1704, V1696, V1630, V1774, V1791, P1388, V1862, V1629, V1779, V1616, V1815, V1855; 297 Squadron—V1851, P1383, V1716, V1769, P1381, P1409, V1864, V1841, V1700, V1852, V1772, P1460, V1812, P1395, V1849, V1858, V1778, V1848, V1868, V1823, V1865, V1825, V1860, V1738, V1861, V1846 and two others.

Preparation for the second phase began as soon as the aircraft had landed, but this had to be postponed as the weather was poor. Indeed, on the morning of 18 September the weather forecast was depressing. Aircrews reported for the 11.45 hours take off but although some of the cloud was as low as 400 feet, marshalling went ahead and the course flown was a repeat of the previous day's. Of 296 Squadron's twenty-one combinations, nineteen released their gliders at the Landing Zone. Flt. Lt. Scott had engine trouble and had to land at Ashford, and Flt. Lt. Horn had aileron trouble. His glider cast off prematurely over Holland. Horn then dived low, seeing the villagers unloading the glider. Of the others in the squadron Flt. Lt. Boyer's machine was hit by flak and its control surfaces were damaged, as he crossed the enemy coast, making the Albemarle difficult to control. He called Flt. Lt. Crokker to help control V1616, then managed to get his glider to the L.Z. and, after a gruelling effort to get back, made a fast landing at Manston. The aircraft which participated in the second phase were: 296 Squadron—V1632 (Wg. Cdr. T. C. Musgrave), V1698, V1774, V1822, V1646, V1696, P1394, V1630, P1391, V1813, V1818, V1853, V1779, V1616, V1785, V1775, V1844, V1704, V1847, V1627; 297 Squadron—P1383, V1823, V1778, V1865, P1395, V1812, V1856, V1846, V1825, V1738, V1864, P1381, V1848 V1769, V1851, V1841 and two with serial numbers unknown.

For the Albemarle the operations of 18 September were virtually its swan song. After their return the crews were informed that they would not be needed on 19 September when the first resupply drops were to be made. Four crews of 296 Squadron flew leaflet-dropping sorties following the Arnhem venture, the last coming on 24 September when pamphlets from V1646 ended the Albemarle's operational career, in this case with 296 Squadron.

Although they were no longer operational, Albemarles continued to play a major part in the airborne forces' activities for they formed the equipment of a number of training and support organizations. The Operational Refresher Training Unit at Hampstead Norris had received its first Albemarles in April 1944 to assist with Horsa and Hadrian flying, relinquishing them in March 1945 when the unit moved to Matching. During that period twenty-three Albemarles served with the unit and participated in operations, V1745 being lost on an operational supply-dropping sortie on 2 July 1944. A small-scale user of Albemarles was the Heavy Glider Conversion Unit at Grove which operated four in the early months of 1943. It made use of another four between August 1944 and its demise, when it was re-organized at North Luffenham in October 1944. From it were born No. 21 Heavy Glider Conversion Unit based at Brize Norton, No. 22 H.G.C.U. based at Keevil and No. 23 H.G.C.U. based at Peplow, all of which used Albemarles. No. 21 H.G.C.U. used them until the end of 1945.

For those who flew in the Albemarles there were many moments to remember. One who made a considerable number of flights from Coventry was J. H. Hartley. His fund of memories commenced with P1363 when the aircraft was being tested—mainly to assess its flying controls—and later as a T.I. aircraft for a torpedo installation. Another aircraft in which he flew was V1600 also used for

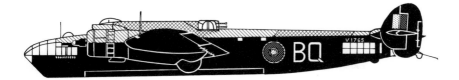

10. An early Albemarle G.T.Mk. V V1765 was delivered direct to 296 Squadron on 31.3.44 and passed to No. 23 H.G.C.U. on 6.11.44. It went to Marshall of Cambridge in February 1945 and was still wearing the depicted markings of 23 H.G.C.U. It left for 5 M.U. in 6.45 where it was struck off charge on 23.4.47. Note the ten light blue parachutes painted on the nose, pale blue identity letters and spinner tips (For key to camouflage colours see page 100)

control checks, particularly for single-engined handling. 'To fly in this aircraft,' he recalls, 'was quite hair-raising until various alterations of rudder trim took place. By that time no one was more pleased than myself when that enormously large propeller started turning again.

'Flying in these aircraft at that time was quite hazardous because of the proximity of the balloon barrage. On one occasion anti-aircraft gunners mistook us for a Dornier and promptly opened fire, luckily missing. Taking off from Baginton was another hazard as one had to be careful not to get tangled in the local barrage balloon cables because, at the time, all test flying was done without radio communication.

'It was also quite an experience to fly in the bomb aimer's position, particularly on landing, as the nosewheel sounded, and felt, as though it was about to land in one's lap. This assembly, on occasions, decided to shimmy violently and this all added to the general excitement.'

But of all the Albemarles to fly in surely none must have been so memorable— other than P1360 with short-span wings—than V1599, the undercarriage of which had long travel to absorb heavy landings. Of this machine J. H. Hartley has vivid memories.

'I flew in V1599 with Mr. C. K. Turner-Hughes, Chief Test Pilot of Armstrong Whitworth, who was responsible for making the first flights of the Albemarle.

20. V1599 was the Albemarle to which long-travel oleo legs were fitted

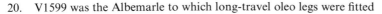

V1599 was converted to use a very long-travel undercarriage. The objects of this were: (i) to reduce the degree of skill required when landing; (ii) to shorten the landing distance by eliminating flatten out and float; and (iii) to make possible landing in conditions of bad visibility. For the last reason the aircraft served later at the Blind Landing Experimental Unit at Farnborough, Martlesham and Woodbridge.

'Early flight trials showed that the undercarriage was reluctant to close at the first contact with the ground. The aircraft would often run for some short distance with the legs fully extended, giving the impression that it was running on seven-foot stilts, and it needed an application of the brakes to persuade them to close.

'It could be flown "into the ground" at a rate of descent of approximately 21 feet per second calling for three times the energy absorption of a normal undercarriage, and then my energy was reduced three-fold while this procedure was taking place!

'After numerous flight trials, in which I usually acted as Flight Engineer, on 10 May 1944 I went with the aircraft to Farnborough, for trials at the Royal Aircraft Establishment. The pilot was Mr. C. K. Turner-Hughes. As previously stated, radio contact was "taboo". On getting a "green" from the tower, we proceeded to make a somewhat spectacular approach and landing.

'The runway surface at that time appeared to be composed of very polished material and early in the landing run the starboard wheel locked very soon resulting in a burst tyre. Then some violent "machining" took place on the brake drum. The aircraft careered down the runway, smoke billowing out. By the time we finally stopped very little more damage had, fortunately, been done.'

Albemarle production ceased in December 1944. Post-war use of the type was very limited, but some interesting work was carried out, using Albemarles, by Dunlop who fitted their Compacta tyres for trials. In August 1947 all remaining R.A.F. Albemarles were ordered to be struck off charge, the last being P1529, declared surplus to needs on 28 August 1947.

The Albemarle's unhappy career was not really a result of its being an unsuccessful aircraft. Indeed, in one important respect it was a pace-maker for it was the first British combat aircraft to be designed from the outset with a nosewheel undercarriage adopted, in the words of Major J. Lloyd, 'to give greater stability and control on the ground'.

When the aircraft arrived on the scene its lateness belied its surprising efficiency after its complex development period for it was as effective a bomber as the Wellington. Had it come into service in 1940, as planned, it certainly would have played a useful part in the bomber offensive. Instead, its lateness brought the problem of how and where to employ it. When it found a niche the Albemarle performed satisfactorily, although one cannot deny that four-engined aircraft made better glider tugs for they had more power reserves. The final words on the Albemarle are best given by two men who were intimately concerned with it. It fell to Hugh Burroughes to become Works Manager at Hawkesley in 1941 and so he is in the leading position to comment upon the production side.

21. V1599 was one of the last Mk. 1s to be built, and spent much of its active test career in the hands of R.A.E. Farnborough although it flew for part of the time from Martlesham Heath and from Woodbridge

'The Albemarle,' he recalls, 'was the only aircraft where the design and prototype building were carried out in the parent works and then handed over to another firm for them to control the working-drawings, the development, the interchangeability problems and the sub-contracting of all components to a large number of firms of which all but two had no previous experience of aircraft manufacture. This handicap, to my mind, was responsible for 75 per cent of the high cost and long delays. Other causes were: (i) the "indifference" of the Air Staff; (ii) the prolonged uncertainty as to its role; (iii) the critical attitude of Bomber Command arising from (a) the fire risk and (b) its inferior payload. The employment of the wooden Mosquito was a similar task, but it was offset by high performance. We learnt of these things only along the "grapevine". Bearing in mind the long experience of Jimmy Lloyd and his team, I feel quite sure that had the Albemarle remained under the control of the parent firm, the structure weight would have been reduced and the criticism of its "low" payload laid low. There is plenty of evidence to show that as soon as a worthwhile role was established and made known to main and sub-contractors alike, the production rate was greatly improved.'

During the development phase the Albemarle team was headed by Mr. C. F. Joy, probably best known for his work on the famous Victor bomber. 'The problems of Albemarle development and production were not confined only to the difficulties of component production,' he recalls, 'but few aircraft sub-contractors had the experience of being thrown in at the deep end in the early days of the war.

'But in fact, the non-aircraft industry made an enormous contribution to overall aircraft production, particularly from 1941–2. However, in every other case, the firm concerned was introduced to its task after most of the production "bugs" had been eliminated by the parent company.

'Ironically, this early impact of the Albemarle component production on non-aircraft companies was by no means a complete loss. Many learned the hard way and as a result played a much more enlightened role on later types like the Mosquito.'

Thus, it may well be argued that the Albemarle lived up to the slogan proudly proclaimed on the factory building at the Coventry works, 'Sir W. G. Armstrong Whitworth, Pacemakers of Progress'.

Key to Camouflage Colours

(See diagrams 5, 6, 8, 9, 10)

▨ Dark green   ▦ Yellow

▧ Dark earth   ▤ Dull red

▢ Azure blue   ▨ Blue

▦ Sky

Summary of Albemarle variants

An A.W.A. Type Number was allocated only when an aircraft design was finally laid down for production, the Albemarle being the A.W. 41. The list here shows the Works Numbers allocated to Albemarle variants (not all of which even acquired Works Numbers).

Works No.	Details
208	Albemarle prototype P1360. Hercules HE 1SM
211	Albemarle second prototype P1361. Hercules HE 1SM
212	P1361 with Hercules III. Production models with Dural insert in main spar. 198 examples ordered
213	Experimental version with $2 \times 1,600$ h.p. Wright Cyclone Gr-2600
217	Albemarle Mk. I srs. i. Hercules XI. Previous 198 aircraft updated to this standard. Subsequently Mk. I srs. ii developed to this order
218	Albemarle with experimental long-travel undercarriage, intended to be applied to a Mk. I srs. iii, eventually a Mk. II
219	Mk. I srs. i completely rewired and supplied to U.S.S.R.
—	Armament test-bed with remotely controlled barbettes in rear of engine nacelles. Project only
—	Glider-tug conversion for 38 Wing
221	S.T.I conversion from Mk. I srs. iii
—	G.T.II conversion; Hercules XI originally
222	Mk. IV srs. i V1760 only. Cyclone GR-2600
223	S.T. Mk. V
225	S.T. Mk. VI srs. i
226	G.T. Mk. VI srs. ii

Albemarle production

Contract 816726/38: Prototypes P1360, P1361.

Contract B.40671/39: 168 aircraft laid down as thirty-two Mk. I srs. i, eight S.T.1 srs. i, forty-six G.T.1 srs. ii, fourteen S.T.I srs. ii, twenty-two G.T.I srs. iii, forty-six S.T.I srs. iii. Many conversions and modifications. Apparently finally stabilized as followed: Mk. I srs. i: P1362–1369, P1372–1373, P1375–1376, P1378, P1380–1384, P1386–1394, P1396, P1398–1401; S.T.Mk. I srs. i: P1370–1371, P1374, P1377, P1379, P1385, P1395, P1397; G.T.Mk. I srs. ii: P1402, P1404–1409 (1406 Cyclone engines), P1430–1432, P1434–1446, P1449–1451, P1453, P1458–1471, P1474, P1476–1478, P1501; S.T.Mk. I srs. ii: P1403, P1433, P1447–1448, P1452, P1454–1457, P1472–1473, P1475, P1479, P1500; G.T.Mk. I srs. iii: P1511–1518, P1521–1529, P1550–1553, P1557, P1590–1609; S.T.Mk. I srs. iii: P1502–1510, P1519–1520, P1554–1556, P1558–1569, P1630–1659.

Contract 2975c/20: From an order for 780 only 302 examples were built, there being numerous conversions from the delivery pattern which is listed here: G.T.Mk. I srs. iii: V1598, V1599; G.T.Mk. II (IIa from V1606): V1600–1647, V1694–1723, V1738–1759 (many laid down as S.T.II and some completed as such within these batches); Mk. IV: V1760; S.T.Mk. V: V1761–1787, V1809–1828, V1841–1842; mixed G.T./S.T. VI srs. i: V1843–1885, V1917–1941; V1962–2011, V2025–2039, V2040–2054; G.T.Mk. VI srs. ii: V2067–2068.

Contract B53250/C20A: 100 G.T.Mk. VI srs. ii: LV482–501, LV532–577, LV590–623.

22. Too good to replace, the trusty Sunderland

Part Three

A Sunderland Replacement: The Short Shetland and the British Military Flying-Boat Development Programme 1938–1953

Live upon an island and one is dependent upon waterborne supplies. Despite the development of the aeroplane, shipping remains the principal means of supply both of food and materials. Aircraft play a supporting role by protecting shipping in time of conflict. An aeroplane able to operate from water was a logical development. Small aircraft could, by the addition of floats, be readily adapted for waterborne operation, but larger machines required the development of suitable hulls. These needed not only to be watertight but also to offer buoyancy and have lift qualities while embodying the considerable strength required on the take-off run and upon landing when the forces encountered would be considerable.

Planing surfaces inevitably increased drag, slowing the aircraft. Thus, required engine power was considerable and flying controls needed to be of sufficient area to ensure adequate manoeuvrability of the craft afloat as well as in the air. Since the hull was required to plane it had to be of chine form embodying a step. The mainplane had to be well clear of the water to protect engines and propellers from spray. The tail needed to be high set for the same reason. Two basic parameters for design revolved around power-loading and wing-loading, but it was noticeable that with increasing size of boats there was a tendency towards increased wing-loadings and decreased power-loadings, accompanied by a decrease in parasitic drag due to cleaning of excrescences.

Being slower than landplanes, military flying-boats needed strong defensive armament which, in turn, increased weight and reduced offensive load. Possible crew fatigue needed to be guarded against, but the addition of a slip crew added to the load factor for it also led to the need for rest bunks and meals provision.

There were factors in favour of and against the employment of flying-boats by the Royal Air Force. Overseas the lack of airfields promoted the flying-boat's value, and with island territories to maintain and much need for ocean surveillance it seemed ideal. Then came the 1939–45 war and with it the building of sophisticated airfields, many with hard-surface runways for heavy aircraft. By 1945 the days of flying-boats were largely over, for land-based aircraft could perform on ocean patrol as well as any flying-boats. Fitting of turbo-prop or jet engines to large boats could not promote them to superiority over landplanes. Military aviation will, however, offer no vista to eclipse the mighty majesty of the large flying-boats. The beauty of a long frothy wake, the excitement of spray spewing high, the ease of wandering freely in a giant hull or just merely gazing at such beautiful craft—all surely brought the most delectable moments in military aviation history.

A wide range of seaplanes was designed for the R.A.F. over a period of thirty years, and their usefulness for ocean patrol cannot be denied. Much of their payload was devoted to fuel, affording them not only long range but, more important, long endurance essential for the open-sea duties of reconnaissance and convoy escort.

Seaplanes could land in sheltered, natural inlets which were often free from obstruction. They could operate from virtually unprepared sites, and when in trouble often find sanctuary on suitable stretches of water. Indeed, there were many instances of them putting down on the open ocean and staying afloat for hours. As the size of landplanes increased, their need for long runways—expensive to build and requiring sites needing careful preparation and selection from the aspects of terrain, weather and population density—gave some confirmation to the value of flying-boats. But their fate was sealed when the American B-24 Liberator joined the R.A.F. and had sufficient range to close the Atlantic gap, and furthermore when the Avro Shackleton, derived from the Lancaster, became available. In considering the Shetland, the last of the line of flying-boats for the R.A.F. to fly, all these aspects feature.

The R.3/38 and the R.5/39 specifications

Even before the war there were those in the Service who considered that the flying-boat should be removed from its inventory, but seaplanes served in small numbers to the outbreak of conflict, at home and overseas. The 1930s brought the first monoplane variety with advances in speed, range and general efficiency of which the Short Sunderland was the prime example. Yet, even as it was being introduced to service, plans were initiated for a successor, the R.3/38. The Sunderland was a 1933 design, much influenced by the successful 'C-Class' Empire Flying-Boats, and made its first flight on 16 October 1937. It entered service in a surprisingly short time, the first being passed to the R.A.F. in May 1938.

The R.3/38 was planned to embody experience already to hand with the new Short boats, and when the preliminary committee meeting was held on 7 July 1938 to consider this next flying-boat design the requirement, in the interest of economy, was for the smallest aircraft which could meet the need. Preference was for a four-engined machine. Although this would need more maintenance its reliability would be better. Air-cooled engines were preferred, but liquid-cooled power plants were acceptable. This flying-boat was to be easily maintained afloat, thus reducing wastage of time and effort beaching the craft, often for small items needing attention. Absence of a turret would make for a streamlined nose, affording improved view for pilots and bomb aimers while raising the aircraft's speed which should equate to that of a shipboard fighter.

The plans were for this aircraft to become standard equipment of all flying-boat squadrons at home and overseas. To enhance its value as a bomber two-speed engine superchargers were required, giving maximum power output at 5,000 and 15,000 feet. If conventional wing-tip floats were selected then these needed to be retractable. Stub wings might, however, suffice. No fuel would be carried in the hull. A midships power-operated turret would mount two 20 mm. Hispano 'long guns', alias cannon, or four ·303 in. Brownings. The latter type would also be fitted in the tail turret. The Sunderland's bomb racks took considerable time to be wound out from the hull. In this replacement aircraft bomb cells would be in the mainplanes. A crew of eight would be composed of the captain and navigator both being pilots, an air observer, two W/T operators, two fitters and an armourer. All-up weight would be about 45,000 lb., range with reconnaissance load 1,500 miles at 235 m.p.h. at economical cruise power. Reinforcing range would be 4,000 miles. There would be provision for a 4,000 lb. bomb load comprising 16×250 lb. or 8×500 lb. G.P., A.S. or 'B' bombs. This offensive load would be less important than the reconnaissance capability.

The draft specification was considered by the Operational Requirements Committee on 29 July 1938. The Commander-in-Chief, Coastal Command, considered the scheme good, but he was concerned about the top speed of the design and thought a maximum of 250 knots (288 m.p.h.) possible with a boat of this size. This was too optimistic and the specification went forward based on a top speed of 235 m.p.h. at 5,000 ft. Coastal Command wanted range to be increased by 2,000 miles, assessed as feasible in an overload condition. Normal tankage would afford a range of 3,000 miles cruising, 4,000 miles at most economic speed, and bombs would have to represent either an increased or alternative loading. A specification embodying these and the foregoing features was issued to Blackburn, Saunders-Roe, Short Bros. and Supermarine on 21 September 1938. By way of comparison the Sunderland I had an all-up weight of around 45,000 lb. and cruised at 115 knots for 12 hours. Its armament comprised nose and tail turrets, two dorsal guns and bombs carried in the fuselage. Thus, R.3/38 represented a streamlined, updated Sunderland.

Ideas from the firms were reviewed during the final three months of 1938 and revealed general weakness in defensive armament. The Air Staff were very disturbed about this and decided that none of the designs was acceptable, completely revised the specification and reissued it to the industry on 31 March 1939 as R.5/39.

Uncertain of the effectiveness of ·303 in. guns, the Air Staff chose four 20 mm. Hispano cannon for a huge hydraulically operated midships gun turret and one 20 mm. cannon to be placed on a pillar mounting in the extreme tail. Heavy dorsal armament disposed of criticism arising from the lack of nose turret because the turret was to be so designed as to be made to depress 10° below horizontal when firing forward. Because of its weight the turret had to be sited over the c.g. Interrupter gear had to be fitted to prevent hits on the propellers. One of the normal crew would load the ammunition into the cannon, and the turret was to be designed to permit fitting of predictor sights later, and possibly two 40 mm. cannon. Automatic feed would place thirty-round ammunition drums in position in the turret, the shape of which had to cause no more than 5 per cent additional drag at top speed. Turrets for prototypes would be acquired on embodiment loan from Boulton Paul, their constructor, who would test the turret on a special prototype aircraft. Tenders for R.5/39 had to be submitted by 27 June 1939.

Four companies returned schemes and figures relating to flying-boats, and the dimensions and performance varied considerably. In the case of their weights, these were already heavier than would have been the case for R.3/38 because of heavy turret armament. The table opposite shows the variations in the projected designs.

Each design was examined by the Royal Aircraft Establishment. All had a high wing-layout. Supermarine's design, which attracted most favour, had twin fins and rudders, wing-tip floats and featured a retractable hull main step. Although novel, its depth of about $4\frac{1}{2}$ inches was half of what would be needed for a hull beam of 9 feet. Hydrofoils with flat bases served as wing floats, their manner of retraction being unsatisfactory. Another unusual feature was a ducted engine-cooling system from which air was bled over the undersurfaces of the wing. Engine heating during taxiing seemed likely to bring disadvantages.

Saunders-Roe had updated their S.38 design, a twin-finned aircraft, the most unusual feature of which was the method of retracting the wing-tip floats. These were split vertically and hinged at their base. Part of the aircraft's fuel load was carried in the hull, and this was unacceptable. Various aircraft had been schemed by the company to R.5/39 and early in 1939 the design was stabilized around the Hercules engine. Overloaded to 67,000 lb., the latest design should have a range of up to 4,000 miles.

Short's contender had a single fin and rudder and, despite the specification's suggestion, had fixed wing-tip floats. In appearance it resembled a Sunderland with a short fairing behind the main step deemed likely to bring about poor water stability.

The other design came from Blackburn, again a twin-finned machine with retractable wing-tip floats. Its internal layout was inferior to that of other designs and bomb stowage particularly unacceptable. It was a general development of the Blackburn B-20 (to Specification R.1/36).

A conference to consider the four designs was held on 28 July 1939. All were well above 45,000 lb. in gross weight—somewhere between 55,000–63,000 lb. seemed average. This was due to increased armament and armour weight since R.3/38 was devised. It had brought about a need for extra engine power, the Bristol Taurus in mind for R.3/38 being insufficiently powerful. Now, the Bristol Hercules (with the Rolls-Royce Griffon as alternative) was the chosen power plant. A need for high speed had much influenced the designers and range seemed

ENGINES	Supermarine *Hercules HE1 SM*	Saunders-Roe *Hercules HE1 SM* (all, alternatively Rolls-Royce Griffon)	Short *Hercules HE1 SM*	Blackburn B.39 *Hercules HE1 SM*
HERCULES				
Maximum speed	323 m.p.h. at 17,000 ft. 293 m.p.h. at 5,000 ft.	284 m.p.h. at 15,000 ft. 273 m.p.h. at 5,000 ft.	279 m.p.h. at 15,000 ft. 260 m.p.h. at 3,500 ft.	299 m.p.h. at 15,000 ft.
Cruising speed	268 m.p.h. at 5,000 ft.	258 m.p.h. at 15,000 ft. 248 m.p.h. at 5,000 ft.	236 m.p.h. at 15,000 ft. 219 m.p.h. at 5,000 ft.	262 m.p.h. at 2,000 ft.
Take-off, weight normal	860 yd.	940 yd.	885 yd.	440 yd.
Landing, normal	820 yd.	680 yd.	980 yd.	550 yd.
Rate of climb, weight normal	3·6 min. to 5,000 ft.	3·2 min. to 5,000 ft.	1,470 f.p.m. at sea level	1,780 f.p.m. at sea level
Normal all-up weight	49,890 lb.	54,935 lb.	60,700 lb.	52,500 lb.
Maximum all-up weight	63,690 lb.	68,885 lb.	71,800 lb.	65,428 lb.
GRIFFON				
Maximum speed	326 m.p.h. at 15,000 ft. 296 m.p.h. at 5,000 ft.	291 m.p.h. at 15,000 ft.	271 m.p.h. at 8,600 ft.	304 m.p.h. at 15,000 ft.
Cruising speed	250 m.p.h. at 5,000 ft.	268 m.p.h. at 15,000 ft. 238 m.p.h. at 5,000 ft.	248 m.p.h. at 19,200 ft.	275 m.p.h. at 6,400 ft.
Normal all-up weight	49,710 lb.	—?—	61,860 lb.	53,550 lb.
Maximum all-up weight	65,610 lb.	—?—	73,290 lb.	66,778 lb.
Wing span	97 ft.	110 ft.	115 ft.	102 ft.
Length	82 ft. 9 in.	97 ft.	94 ft.	85 ft. 7 in.
Height	—?—	27 ft. 9 in.	26 ft.	22 ft.
Draught	3 ft. 10½ in.	4 ft. 6 in.	4 ft. 9 in.	4 ft. 5 in.
Normal wing-loading (Hercules)	36·7 lb./sq. ft.	33·5 lb./sq. ft.	33·9 lb./sq. ft.	31·8 lb./sq. ft.

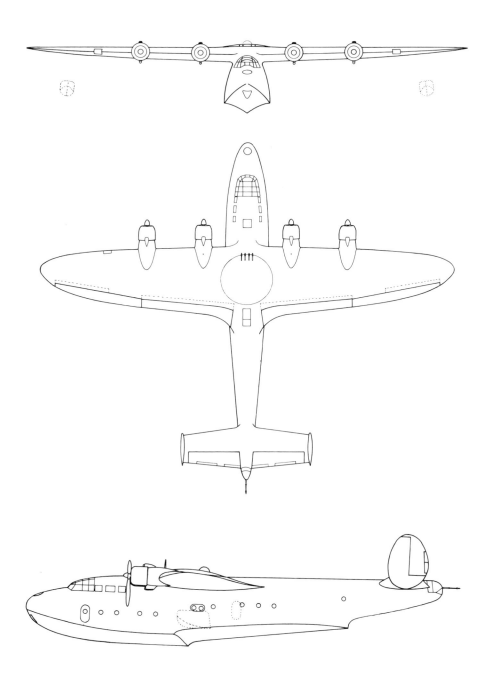

11.   General arrangement of the Saunders-Roe project to Specification R.5/39

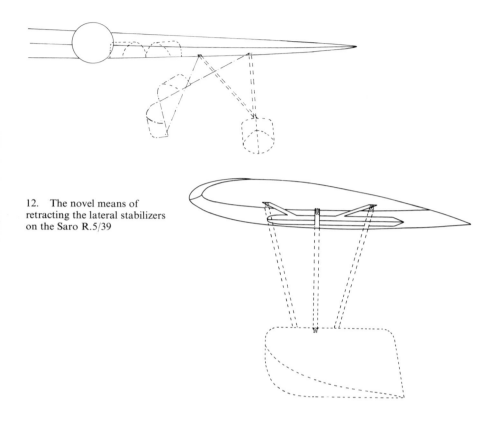

12. The novel means of
retracting the lateral stabilizers
on the Saro R.5/39

likely to have suffered. Heavier engines and the large dorsal turret had produced
a flying-boat equivalent of the important B.1/39 bomber.

A draught of not more than 4 feet had been specified, but except for the
Supermarine design the size of the flying-boat had brought the draught beyond 4
feet at a time when there was uncertainty about the behaviour on take off of boats
with considerable draught. Satisfactory gun depression in the forward plane
could be achieved by only the Short and Saro designs. There was the possibility
that a submarine might be engaged on an approach to attack, but the extent of
cannon effectiveness was not known. Twin fins were preferable because they
permitted a better field of fire against attack from astern. Short's design was
therefore unpopular because of the single fin and rudder, and also because of
fixed floats. Supermarine's design had a very large well into which floats would
have to retract. This seemed likely to weaken considerably the wing structure.
Nevertheless the Supermarine design was the best, with the Saunders-Roe
project a fairly close second although its integral wing tanks were unacceptable.
However, Supermarine's retractable-step idea would need much development.

Saunders-Roe had stolen a major advance over their competitors. In February 1939 they decided to build a scale model of their R.5/39 design, designated A.37. It was intended to furnish data on hull and aerodynamic design. Experience with the water characteristics of the Lerwick indicated a comparatively large-scale effect on stability on the water as well as in running attitude, resistance and moments. A half-scale model was considered sufficiently near to full scale for accurate forecasting of water behaviour. Following tank tests on the R.A.E. high-speed tank, design work began on the model. The 50-foot span A.37 two-seater was powered by four Pobjoy Niagara III engines and had a plywood wing. Registered in August 1939 as G-AFZS and commonly called the 'Shrimp', it first flew in October 1939, by which time the flying-boat programme had trodden a tortuous path.

The designers had clearly been optimistic about speeds and structure weights of the R.5/39 projects, except for Short's scheme. All designs, it was forecast, would fail to meet take-off and landing requirements, and the Supermarine design would need larger propellers to improve its take off. On the time factor, Supermarine stated that they could be ready to start work within three months, Saunders-Roe immediately, but neither aircraft would be available in less than three years.

In August 1939 it was decided that the Supermarine design should go ahead, but with the unusual Saro wing floats, and with additional wing area. Inboard engines would be sited slightly outwards to permit the fitting of 14 ft. 6 in. diameter propellers. Hull beam and step depth relationships would need further investigation. Although the Short design looked dependable, because Saro were building the half-scale model at their own expense it was decided instead to order the Saro S.38 also, if the firm would first agree to redesign the spars.

Along with these decisions came a totally new proposal, for the Sunderland Mk. II — not in any way to be confused with the Sunderland Mk. II of later years. Power plants would be Rolls-Royce Merlin RM2 SM. The wing would be strengthened, the forward fuselage more streamlined and the beam increased. Extra fuel would be carried and the hull base would have to be strengthened because of the aircraft's greater weight and higher stalling speed. Cannon armament might be featured, as on the Stirling II. Compared to the early Sunderland the project Mk. II had the features shown in the table on p. 112. Thus, somewhat of an about turn had been made towards R.3/38; towards the original idea for a smaller flying-boat of which about fifty or sixty were needed.

Against such a design was the fact that Short Bros. were busy with the Stirling. Their productive capacity would soon be well stretched. Yet in mid-August 1939 the Director of Technical Development came forward with a totally new concept that was eventually to alter the flying-boat programme completely. Short Bros., he suggested, with all their flying-boat expertise to draw upon, should design an ultra-large flying-boat. Its function would be decided as its technical prospects became clearer. Unwittingly, Mr. W. S. Farren, later Sir William Farren, had set in motion the plan which would result in the post-war Saro Princess. Ironically, it was his opinion at this time that Saro would be unable to carry out a task as large

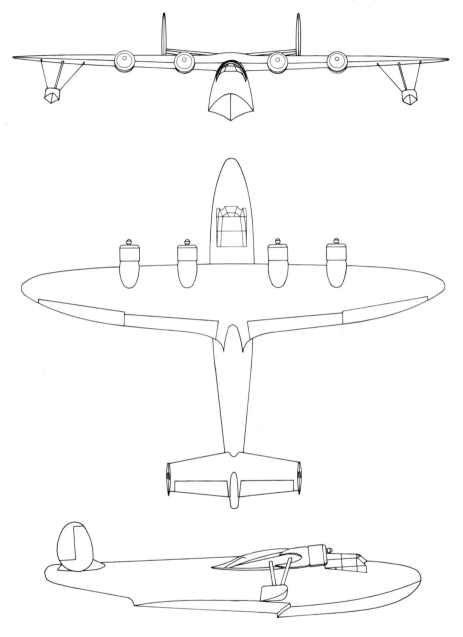

13.   Saro 37 'Shrimp' layout. Salient dimensions: Wing span 50 ft., overall length 42 ft. $3\frac{1}{4}$ in., overall height 12 ft. $8\frac{3}{4}$ in., wing area 340 sq. ft., aileron area (1) 14.2 sq. ft., flap area (1) 18.1 sq. ft., tailplane area 43.2 sq. ft., elevator area (1) 10.7 sq. ft., fin area (1) 11.5 sq. ft., rudder area (1) 6.7 sq. ft.

	Mk. I	Mk. II Project
Normal all-up weight (lb.)	44,670	52,800
Maximum speed (m.p.h.)		
5,000 ft.	211	245
15,000 ft.	198	252
Maximum economic cruise speed		
5,000 ft	178	225
15,000 ft.	160	232
Range (land miles)	1,780	1,780
Overload weight (lb.)	50,000	55,800
Overload range (miles)	2,900	2,900

23.   G-AFZS, the Saro Shrimp half-scale model of the R.5/39, during a wartime test flight

as he had in mind for Short's, although he considered Saro to be 'ambitious'. He felt that they lacked the knowledge for such a demanding programme, and thought that they should concentrate upon making the Lerwick a success, which he thought to be possible. This notion of a large flying-boat was left on one side for some months because the outbreak of war turned attention towards less exotic and more useful ideas, but September 1939 was a time of fast decision where the flying-boat programme was concerned. In the middle of that month the Air Staff abruptly decided to halt the R.5/39 programme because of its long time scale.

At a meeting of the Experimental Aircraft Programme Committee on 4 October 1939 it was stated that the Air Staff no longer wanted a Sunderland replacement. That design was adequate, and could be updated in the normal course of events. As far as Short, Blackburn and Supermarine were concerned that marked the end of R.5/39, but Saro—with commendable foresight—considered that a replacement would eventually be required and continued their design work as a private venture.

The early development of the Short Shetland and the Blackburn R.13/40

Not wishing to lose the £100,000 allocated for R.5/39, Air Ministry decided to switch funding to general flying-boat development, in particular towards smaller flying-boats. The Air Staff's view, however, was that if a crew of eight was required then no smaller boat could emerge. Nevertheless they acquiesced to consideration of smaller flying-boats carrying a crew of less than eight.

During December 1939 the Director of Operational Requirements stated that the minimum range acceptable for any flying-boat was 2,500 miles at normal operational load, 3,000 miles without bombs. But the fundamental issue still surrounded speed. If 120 m.p.h. was acceptable for cruising, then the required range could be achieved by some reduction of crew and accommodation. A cruising speed of 200 m.p.h. seemed likely to result in a boat larger than the Sunderland. Then, on 4 December 1939, a statement was made to the effect that the Sunderland was considered well able to meet all requirements likely to be needed during the war. This indeed turned out to be the case, although its range was somewhat insufficient by the mid-war period Atlantic patrols. With modified step, improved armament and engine changes it served the Royal Air Force for almost twenty years. Coastal Command only used the American Catalina when the Sunderland was in short supply.

It was also in December 1939 that the Director of Operations (Naval Command) was asked for an outline of his needs. He requested a flying-boat with a range of 2,500 nautical miles with 2,000 lb. bomb load, or 3,000 nautical miles without bombs. Maximum speed should, he felt, be 220 knots (253 m.p.h.), cruising speed 180 knots (207 m.p.h.), economic cruising speed 120–150 knots.

Nose and tail turrets should carry defensive armament and the crew number eight. He thus advocated an aircraft akin to the cancelled R.5/39.

If such a machine was needed then what should now be done? Cessation of the development of new flying-boats was disturbing to some officials, particularly those with an eye to post-war civil aviation. They could see that competitive American flying-boats were improving fast in the civil field, and could be a commercial threat to British designs. The Air Staff felt that the best policy would be to produce a new Sunderland variant with increased range, for the latter had now assumed greater importance in their thinking than speed. Raising the Sunderland's all-up weight from 51,000 lb. to 56,000 lb. would allow for an additional 500 gallons of fuel, improved hull design and power-operated bomb-rack traversing gear to speed the racks' passage from the hull. Retractable floats could be fitted and twin fins to reduce swing on take off.

Some had been uneasy at the cancellation of R.5/39, which would have been able to do much more than a modified Sunderland. It was these people who suggested that an American design might serve in place of R.5/39. This machine was the Consolidated PB2Y Coronado, first delivered to the U.S. Navy for trials in the autumn of 1938. In the form in which it was to be supplied to the U.S. Navy, it was believed that delivery to the Royal Air Force could begin in nine months' time, which was over optimistic. To have acquired one example and equipped it in the manner of R.5/39 would have taken twenty months. A third possibility was for Saro to acquire a licence to build this aircraft.

During December the idea of taking an American design was pursued, although no firm information about the capabilities of the PB2Y were to hand. It was Mr. W. S. Farren's opinion that to buy the American boat could be a very wrong decision with serious implications for the future. He again suggested that Short Bros. plan a 160,000 lb. flying-boat, assess likely performance and capability for both military and civil use, and estimate time needed to produce a half-scale model as well as the full-sized machine.

The Commander-in-Chief, Coastal Command, had always been concerned at the abandonment of R.5/39. On 13 January 1940, when urging continuance of British flying-boat development, he put forward suggestions for a new design with the much increased all-up weight of 84,000 lb. He wanted a bomb load of 4,000 lb., normal range with offensive load of 2,500 sea miles and a cruising speed of not less than 200 knots with an economic cruise speed of 170 knots. He wanted four guns in dorsal and tail turrets, and a crew of nine. He was advocating a much scaled-up Sunderland.

At the start of February, figures relating to the Consolidated PB2Y were received and a simple comparison between this and the now defunct R.5/39 was drawn up as shown in the following table.

The American boats would cost $1 million each, and delivery could start in a year's time. Only in respect of maximum speed—now judged of secondary importance to range—did R.5/39 appear to better the American machine which was already flying. But more was at stake than merely one design: indeed, the whole future of the British flying-boat, of which no new design was being

	PB2Y	*R.5/39*
Gross weight (lb.)	66,000	75,000
Maximum wing-loading (lb./sq. ft.)	37	45·5
Range at 5,000 ft. (miles)	4,000	4,000
	at 175 m.p.h.	at 178 m.p.h.
Maximum speed (m.p.h.)	232	272

officially supported. Therefore a week later, in a complete about turn, it was decided yet again to consider R.5/39 in relation to ideas for a much smaller flying-boat, and that an improved Sunderland should once more be looked at.

A list of the bewildering number of suggestions for new flying-boats was drawn up by the Director of Operational Requirements on 29 February 1940. The PB2Y was now out of favour, leaving a new small flying-boat, the R.5/39, an 84,000 lb. boat, an improved Sunderland, an Air Ministry inspired curious idea for a flying-boat powered by six small engines, and the giant pet of the Director of Technical Development. Not all could go forward, but . . . which should?

Of these designs the improved Sunderland would match the needs for the proposed small boat but not meet the new Coastal Command requirements. The Director of Research and Development recommended development of an improved Sunderland to keep that design effective while, for the future, giving a free hand to D.T.D. 'to keep flying-boat design alive in whatever manner it was considered would result in the greatest benefit to the Services and industry'. The D.T.D.'s opinion had now completely veered towards a very large flying-boat. The Short Shetland was thus being conceived or, rather, being allowed to creep into being without the R.A.F. requesting it.

In late March 1940, the Director of Naval Operations maintained that the Sunderland should be developed, carrying increased loads or having additional range without speed alteration. He considered that if his ideas of December 1939 could not be met in a small flying-boat then one of up to 20 tons, and another of 25–30 tons to equate Coastal Command's needs, should be produced. To him also range was now the most important item, and he was willing to accept a speed as low as 120 knots (138 m.p.h.) for cruising. He felt that C-in-C Coastal Command's speed requirements were too high. Twin-engined machines might well suffice, but the Director of Naval Operations also suggested that 'a larger boat should be designed with a view to its use as a civil aircraft after the war'. Now he, too, was supporting the idea which became the Shetland.

Yet another review of the existing flying-boat programme was made on 11 April 1940. The increasing number of schemes and lack of decision was now profoundly disturbing. Opinion was strongly in favour of the aircraft with the greatest range, but just what could be achieved? Many of the accruing problems would have disappeared had range been set at 2,500 miles and a moderate-sized general-purpose boat built.

There were at this time plans for five types of flying-boat: (a) a Sunderland Mk. II being developed to the needs of D.N.O. and the Air Staff; (b) the specification from D.T.D. for a large aircraft to keep flying-boat development alive and upon which there was as yet little general agreement; (c) a revised idea of R.5/39 with an all-up weight of 50,000/60,000 lb.; (d) the Coastal Command suggestion for a boat of 84,000 lb.; and (e) a specification being devised for a small boat which would perform better than the Sunderland, suggesting that it could not be all that small. A range of 4,250 miles had been suggested, for a design based upon the PBY-5. A speed of 120 m.p.h. for cruise was suggested, linked to an astonishing thirty-six hours' duration capability. Details of these schemes are shown in the following table.

	Revised R.5/39	Small boat	Sunderland II	Coastal Command spec.
Maximum weight (lb.)	102,500	55,000	56,000	84,000
Range (miles):				
with bombs	3,550	3,000	3,100	2,880
no bombs	4,000	3,500	3,450	— ?—
Economic speed (m.p.h.):				
5,000 ft.	160	132	141	196
Maximum speed (m.p.h.):				
15,000 ft.	297	238	218	230
5,000 ft.	280	230	207	— ?—
Bomb load (lb.)	4,000	2,000	2,000	2,000
Crew	8	8	7	9
Armament	1 cannon tail	4 machine gun tail	4 machine gun tail	4 machine gun tail
	4 cannon dorsal	2 machine gun nose	2 machine gun dorsal	4 machine gun dorsal
			2 machine gun bow	

The ever-increasing complexity of the flying-boat programme was further reviewed at a meeting on 17 April 1940. The D.D.R.A. reported that a lot of work had been completed on an improved Sunderland, making take off possible at about 55,000 lb. all-up weight. Further advance would only come about by utilizing the new untried Bristol Centaurus engine, and lead to a flying-boat of about 100,000 lb. gross weight. A range of 4,000 sea miles would then be possible,

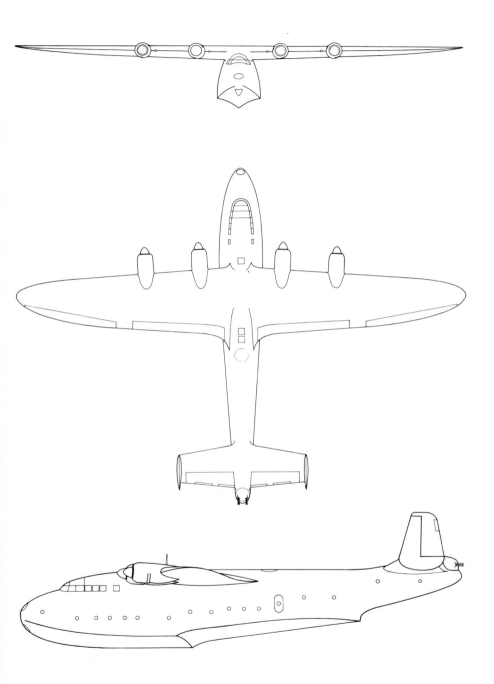

14.   Saro Project 39 of April 1940

but the suggested cannon turrets might induce too much drag for this to be achieved. Another opinion was that any other combination of engine/size would not be able to offer the range Coastal Command desired, and that the Sunderland's range would remain insufficient for the future.

Although he had suggested forging ahead with a large flying-boat with civil possibilities, the D.N.O. re-emphasized the value of small flying-boats, especially from the production point of view. He still wanted such machines cruising at 120 m.p.h. and with an armed range of 2,500 sea miles. But a majority at the meeting was against small boats.

Knowing of Coastal Command's interest in a flying-boat larger than the original 5.5/39, Saunders-Roe designed their S.39 with a normal all-up weight of 80,000 lb. Its top speed was projected as 300 m.p.h. at 15,000 ft. Like the S.38A it had an overload weight of 96,000 lb. for which an optimistic range of 5,000 miles was forecast. But this design straddled the present requirements. A further design drawn up in April 1940 featured two Frazer-Nash dorsal gun turrets and had provision for a bomb load of 8,000 lb. for short-range operations and was thus carrying some features which would be called for from the projected large flying-boat to which it soon became related.

By late April the choice of projects to follow was reduced to three. On 24 April 1940 the Director General of Research and Development held a meeting to discuss: (a) the Sunderland replacement; (b) a six-engined flying-boat; and (c) a small flying-boat. Plans for the first of these, which it was now clear should have been decided upon when the Sunderland first entered service, were now quite outdated particularly in comparison with American flying-boats. The remedy suggested now was to update R.5/39 and increase its engine power by using Napier Sabre or Bristol Centaurus engines. Certainly the all-up weight would rise dramatically, from 65,000 lb. to 100,000 lb. But performance would be much superior, also armament and offensive load. This new R.5/39 would have an all-up weight 50 per cent greater at maximum overload than the earlier one, logically follow on from Short's new G-Class boat and be very suitable for adaptation as a civil trans-Atlantic airliner.

It was now decided to commission a revised R.5/39 from Saunders-Roe who would produce a design study for a civil boat too. Having kept alive their interest in a machine of this type, they were able, by the end of April 1940, to offer the S.38A which had an all-up weight of 62,000 lb. and a top speed of 285 m.p.h. at 15,000 ft. In overloaded state and weighing 96,000 lb. the projected range was 3,500 miles. The revised R.5/39 design had a retractable four-gun turret amidships, a tail turret and could, on short range sorties, carry a 4,000 lb. bomb load.

Concerning the second item discussed on 24 April 1940 it was agreed to produce a 100,000 lb. 'scale model' of a 190,000 lb. flying-boat for military use. Some of the committee pressed for a civil equivalent with an all-up weight of 185,000 lb. to carry sleeping facilities for fifty passengers and 9,000 lb. of mail or freight, and to operate on the Southampton–New York run. The D.G.R.D., too, pressed for this huge machine to go forward as a civil project, but the consensus at the meeting was for a military machine only, though it was decided to include a civil variant when drawing up a specification. Plans would revolve around an aircraft with the features listed in the following table.

	Case A	*Case B*	*Civil type*
All-up weight (lb.)	155,800	157,340	185,000
Bomb load (lb.)	18,000	18,000	9,000 (freight)
Engines	6 Centaurus	6 Centaurus	6 Centaurus
Fuel (gal.)	4,030	4,150	9,000
Armament	4 cannon amidships 2 cannon in each wing turret	2 cannon amidships 2 × ·50 in. guns in each wing turret 4 × ·50 in. tail guns	Nil
Crew	14	14	10
Maximum speed (m.p.h.)	320 at 25,000 ft.	311 at 25,000 ft.	275 at 10,000 ft.
Range (miles)	2,000 at 265 m.p.h.	2,000 at 255 m.p.h.	3,850 at 208 m.p.h. (40 m.p.h. headwind)
Overloaded:			
weight (lb.)	190,000	190,000	—?—
fuel (gal.)	8,560	8,510	—?—
Maximum range (miles)	4,466 at 220 m.p.h.	4,420 at 220 m.p.h.	—?—

To placate D.N.O.'s repeated desire for smaller boats it was proposed that there be development of the unconventional Blackburn R.1/36 which had a retractable hull-planing surface. With twin Sabres or Centaurus, such a machine, based loosely upon the Saro Lerwick and of about 38,000–40,000 lb. all-up weight, would achieve the required speed although range would be reduced since guns and armour comprised a higher percentage of the all-up weight than would be the case with a larger boat.

The Blackburn R.1/36 stemmed from the same specification as the Lerwick. To reduce drag, Major J. D. Rennie had invented a retracting hull-planing area. An all-metal pontoon, which carred 976 gallons of fuel, kept the propellers well clear of the water when in lowered position and maintained sufficient wing incidence for take off. To reduce the drag still further the wing-tip floats were also retractable. Crew stations were commendably spacious, a galley was provided and mooring gear was sited in the pontoon. Four 500 lb. bombs could be carried in the wing centre section. The Saro Lerwick had been favoured because of its greater simplicity and the fear of delay to the Blackburn design. A prototype, V8914, ordered for trial purposes, was built at Blackburn's Dumbarton factory.

The Blackburn R.1/36 first flew in March 1940. Its life was short for it crashed into the Clyde on 7 April 1940. In the hands of the Marine Aircraft Experimental Establishment, the aircraft was being flown by Flt. Lt. H. Bailey when—during top-level speed trials—control was lost as a result of aileron flutter. Consensus was that high speed tests should not have been undertaken as early as that in the flight test programme. The accident happened as opinion was veering away from the revised R.5/39—which was soon dropped—and towards the long-considered large flying-boat. The Deputy Director of Research and Development decided that with a four-Centaurus conventional design the required load would be a better proposition within an overload weight of about 110,000 lb. in the large boat. Improved aerodynamics would permit the 4,000 mile range and offer reasonably good take-off qualities though cruising speed would not be very high. On 25 May 1940 the Director, A.M.D.P., agreed and instructions for the development of this large aircraft were ordered to be issued. Short's and Saro would be invited to prepare designs to a new specification R.14/40 of July 1940. At the same time Blackburn would receive a contract to develop a retractable-pontoon-hull small boat to Specification R.13/40, a specification based on the earlier R.1/36. A range of 1,500 miles at maximum cruising speed at 5,000 ft. was deemed acceptable after all. Overloaded, R.13/40 would have a range of 3,500 miles at a cruising speed of not less than 210 m.p.h. Nose and dorsal turrets would mount two ·303 in. guns, the tail turret four. Bomb load would be 2,000 lb. and D.N.O. would have his small flying-boat after all.

The large R.14/40 was currently viewed merely as an experimental D.T.D./Air Ministry aircraft with advice on the project being given by the Air Staff. Defensive armament would comprise a dorsal turret mounting four 20 mm. cannon and a tail turret carrying four ·50 in. machine guns.

By August 1940, following early design study, it was clear that weight would have to be saved in the large aircraft. Such items as the slinging gear, sub-division of components and carriage of a spare engine and propellers would need considerable thought. Already the armament had been changed to four turrets, each mounting four ·303 in. guns with provision for a later change to ·50 in. guns. The die had been cast and on 24 August, with favour now falling on the Short design, a meeting was held with the firm. It was on this occasion that a somewhat startling notion was revealed—the aircraft was to be treated as a heavy bomber. Short's Chief Designer then claimed that the flying-boat could be designed to carry a 20,000 lb. bomb load, 8,000 lb. of which would be carried in the wings and the remainder traversed from the fuselage as with the Sunderland—if the bombs were limited in calibre to 500 lb. This heavy loading was agreed for a range of 1,000 miles. Because of the position of the dorsal turrets a single fin and rudder were necessary.

Short's proposed reverse-flow engine cooling. It was believed at this time that high-power radial engines could not be cooled sufficiently by the central-entry cooling system, and that reversed-flow cooling was essential. It was claimed that this led to reduced drag because of cleaner cowlings, although there was concern that it could introduce undue complications. However, Bristol would not give agreement to the proposed power output until reversed flow had been tried. It proved too difficult to develop within an acceptable time scale and was dropped in favour of central-entry cooling.

The range of R.14/40 was now set at 3,400 sea miles, overloaded weight 94,000 lb., normal weight 76,000 lb. and most economical cruise speed 135 knots, which indicated a smaller machine than recently proposed. Short Bros. soon presented two schemes, one with a wing-loading of 42 lb. per sq. ft., the other of 48 lb. per sq. ft. The suggested higher wing-loading seemed likely to bring about porpoising and Arthur Gouge of Short's preferred the lower wing-loading. In the Mk. II version of the flying-boat, 20 mm. cannon would be installed in tail and dorsal positions, the nose turret being deleted. All-up weight would rise by 3,000 lb. In reply to a suggestion that a cannon turret could be produced in five months it was stated that even the ·50 in. gun turret would take nine months to develop. In reality neither type of turret became available to the R.A.F. in less than five years.

It is perhaps of interest to record at this point that the retractable-hull idea of Major Rennie also interested Saunders-Roe. They applied the idea to the S.39A, an adaptation of the R.5/39 Spec. to R.14/40. There is no evidence that it was ever submitted for official reaction, and it was a much larger aircraft than R.13/40. It is best looked upon as a natural advance of R.5/39.

In October 1940 Saunders-Roe proposed the S.40 which was a civil version of the S.39 and which it closely resembled as the following table shows.

	S.39	*S.40 civil*
Length (ft.)	105	103
Wing span (ft.)	137	140
Height (ft.)	33	33
Wing area (sq. ft.)	2,200	2,360
Hull beam (ft.)	13	13
Weight empty (lb.)	44,300	47,500

Design work on the Short R.14/40 proceeded along agreed lines. On 1 November 1940 it was decided to provide a heavy armour-plated bulkhead aft of the flight deck wherein the eleven-man crew could take refuge if attacked. This, like every other addition, could but reduce range. At a meeting on 13 November 1940 it was confirmed that only ·50 in. guns could be fitted. Soon after, the reduced bomb load of 18,000 lb. was agreed to, an alternative to a load of the new 1,500 lb. Mk. 5 mines. 'It would be wise', it was stated, 'to accommodate the 8,000 lb. bomb if it can be done', for the aircraft, it will be remembered, was, incredibly, now looked upon as a strategic bomber. Range would be about 3,000 nautical miles but with only a 2,000 lb. bomb load.

A summary of projects in hand was discussed at the Ministry of Aircraft

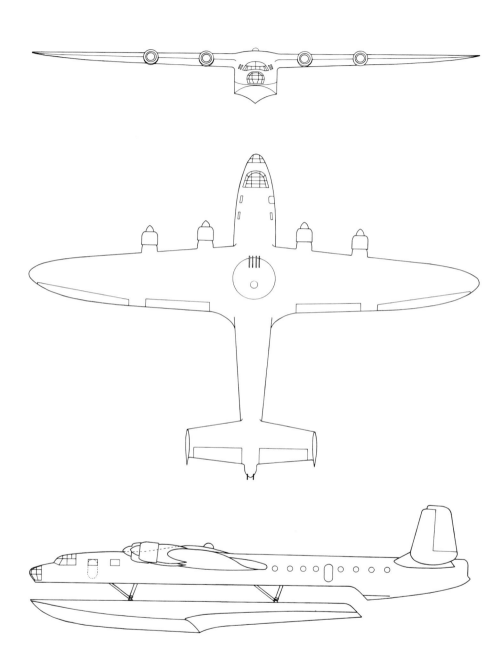

15.   Saro Project 39A (Retractable Hull Planing) of summer 1940

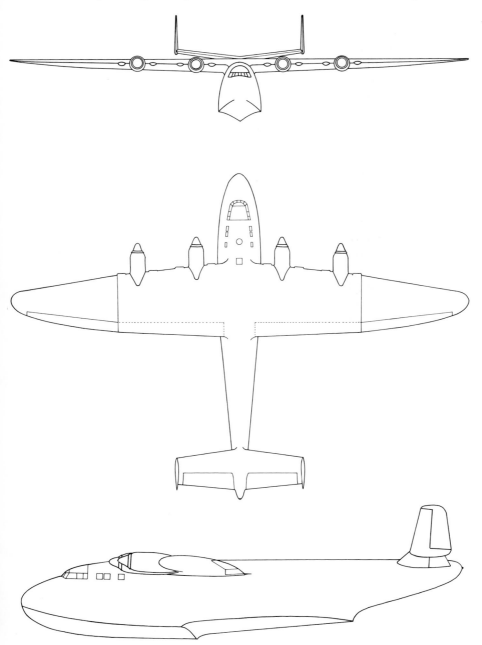

16.   Saro 40 civil flying-boat. Overall length 102 ft., wing span 140 ft., height above base line of fin tip 33 ft.

Production on 18 December 1940. Two designs to R.14/40 were underway by Short's and Saro, the latter having updated their ideas from R.5/39. The Blackburn retractable-hull R.13/40 should be able to replace the Sunderland and offer a much higher speed while retaining the Sunderland's range and better armament. The Director of Technical Development considered that the retractable-pontoon scheme offered an advantage of 30 m.p.h. and some other incidental benefits. Less frontal area and complete step fairing must, in his opinion, reduce drag.

There were rumblings at the meeting from M.A.P. representatives. More important projects were in hand and it was suggested that development of large flying-boats be slowed down, that Short's had their hands full enough making a success of the Stirling. Saro, it was said, had not proved themselves very successful designers for the R.A.F., for the Lerwick had turned out a failure. What importance did the Air Staff attach to the new flying-boats, it was asked. The most optimistic date for completion of the prototype R.13/40 was eighteen months away, Short's R.14/40 about the same time and the Saro design two years. 'It can be argued', said one member at the meeting, 'that none of these boats is likely to be in service in time to affect this war.' But the awaited Air Staff views would outweigh any held by the Ministry of Aircraft Production. The main purpose of the large boat was for long, deep reconnaissance or a lengthy stay on station. Surely, it was suggested, the craft would not be as suitable for a long-range bomber as a land-based aircraft? The corollary was that a landplane, such as the Stirling, could perform the task better. Nevertheless, it was decided that R.14/40 should continue, but be carefully reviewed before any production capacity was set aside for it. It was at this time that the Short design was finally chosen. Two prototypes were now agreed upon and an order for twenty-five or thirty production aircraft was to go ahead, at a production rate of about two per month. The Blackburn R.13/40 would continue, for there was no foreseeable reason why it should not replace the Sunderland.

A policy meeting of 18 February 1941 showed that R.14/40 would make great demands upon skilled labour, and much equipment such as ·50 in. gun turrets and auxiliary power units needed to be designed specifically for the aircraft. It could only proceed at the expense of the Stirling and Sunderland production. The Vice-Chief of the Air Staff said that the R.14/40 programme had been agreed and he thought that it should proceed.

To Coastal Command it seemed a 'terrible indictment' that at such a late date there was still argument about a Sunderland replacement. The Commander-in-Chief felt that the outcome of the war would be decided at sea and 'the best, perhaps only, counter to the U-boats, was the flying-boat. As regards suggestions that a landplane would serve the purpose equally well, the reasons for the superiority of the flying-boat were too many to enumerate.' He mentioned better navigation facilities and greater crew comfort—important psychologically. There was an urgent need for an aircraft to fly 1,000 miles out to sea and operate at this distance for many hours, and R.14/40 would be able to achieve this. In his opinion the flying-boat was essential to a well-balanced airforce. It seemed less

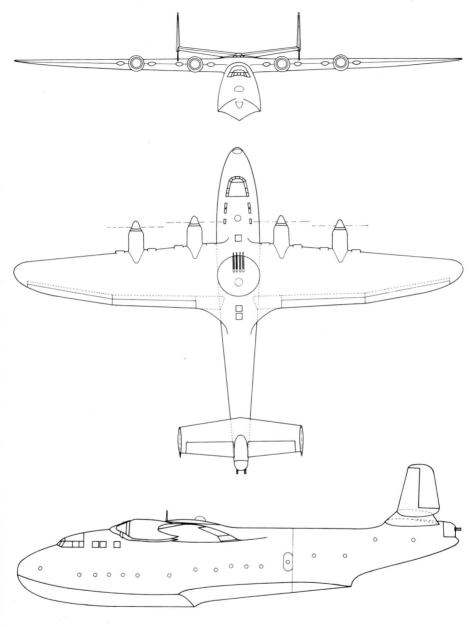

17.   Saro Project 39 (Revised) to Specification R.14/40. Note the four-cannon dorsal turret and the incorporation of reverse-flow cooling for the engines. Wing span 137.5 ft., length overall 101.5 ft., height over fin above base line 34 ft., height over airscrews 22.5 ft., beam 13 ft., wing area 2,200 sq. ft.

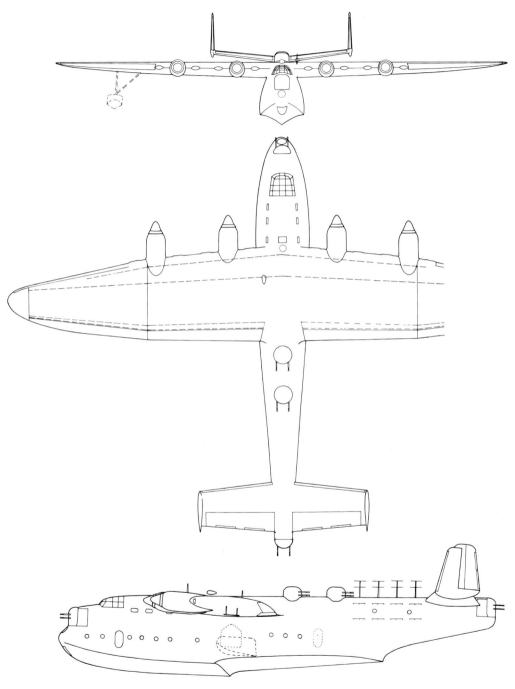

18.   Saro Project to R.14/40 of January 1941 meeting updated requirements

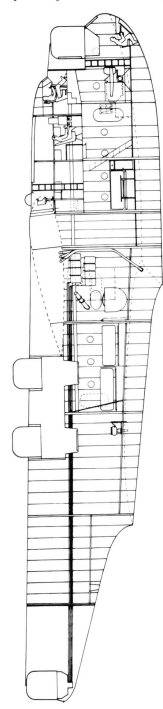

19.   Cut-away of the Saro R.14/40 of January 1941

essential that R.13/40 proceed, but from a trials point of view it was worth continuing. It could do the same work as the Sunderland, more efficiently and faster. It was agreed that it should continue even at the expense of Sunderland production. The Vice-Chief of the Air Staff then agreed that R.14/40 must proceed, and on 3 June 1941 an order for twenty-five to thirty examples was confirmed.

Problems in achieving the required range were already apparent. The 4,000-mile reinforcement range was unlikely to be achieved without a reduction in military load. The latter was reduced by 4,000 lb. as a result of reducing the amount of ammunition carried, deleting one dorsal turret, one radio, the power-operated dinghy and forced-landing flares. Permanent tankage would be increased by about 500 gallons which would replace stowage space of a 1,000 lb. bomb load. The duplication of the auxiliary power unit was to be reviewed. It was then decided to reduce the ammunition load while retaining two dorsal turrets. Owing to its very limited ceiling, the boat could have little value as a bomber.

These changes were ordered in August 1941 when it was also decided that to build twenty-five or thirty examples of the Shetland was impracticable. The order was then amended to two prototypes and ten production aircraft which might be useful as post-war civil transports, since the war seemed likely to be over even before the aircraft were built. Interest in post-war civil aircraft may be considered somewhat curious at this time when the Battle of the Atlantic was not going well, let alone the war in other theatres. The preoccupation in the minds of those in the Ministry of Aircraft Production was how to acquire operational aircraft immediately, and they felt that the Shetland could severely upset Sunderland delivery. It was at this time that a new Commander-in-Chief of Coastal Command was appointed, Air Chief Marshal Sir Philip B. Joubert de la Ferté. His main task was to plan the campaign against the U-boats. He raised an interesting suggestion—that the Shetland could accommodate in the nose a 40 mm. cannon with which to attack them. This, though, would have meant dispensing with forward defence guns, and Italian fighters in particular had, of late, been pressing home frontal attacks on Sunderlands. Countering his interesting suggestion it was argued that a gun duel with a U-boat was undesirable since the large flying-boat offered a vulnerable target which a 40 mm. cannon could not defend.

The increase in all-up weight of the Shetland, which was still rising, brought more concern. On 3 September 1941, the Director of Technical Development visited Rochester to discuss with Short's the structure weight, estimated by the manufacturers as 34,170 lb. and by D.T.D. as 38,500 lb. The all-up weight for stressing purposes had risen to 120,000 lb., so a tabulation was drawn up showing how these estimates related to each other, as shown in the following table.

As a result of the ensuing discussion, D.T.D. informed the Chief of Research and Development and Assistant Chief of the Air Staff that Short's latest estimate for a 4,000-mile range at most economical speed, in normal-load state and without bombs, appeared to be for an aircraft as heavy as 128,000 lb.—whereas

	Short Bros.	RDT.1
Structure (lb.)	34,170	38,500
Armour, de-icing (lb.)	2,090	2,990
Power units (lb.)	21,610	21,600
Equipment and crew (lb.)	17,570	19,620
Weight equipped (lb.)	75,440	82,710
Fuel (lb.)	39,900	35,750
Oil (lb.)	2,660	1,540
Total weight (lb.)	118,000	120,000
Performance estimates:		
range (miles)	4,000	3,000
For reinforcing:		
delete (lb.)	4,000	5,200
add (lb.)	— ?—	— ?—
Equipped for reinforcing (lb.)	71,440	78,790
Fuel (lb.)	39,000	39,410
Oil (lb.)	2,660	1,800
Total reinforcing weight (lb.)	114,000	120,000
Reinforcing range (miles)	4,000	3,500

the maximum weight which was acceptable for occasional operations was 120,000 lb. For general operations it was 110,000 lb. Some drastic changes in military load were therefore essential. The aim was to make 110,000 lb. the limit, allowing for unforeseen demands arising during development. It was now agreed by A.C.A.S.(T) that the dorsal turret (2,690 lb.) should be deleted, raising range by 120 miles. Operational ceiling would be 10,000 ft. so the oxygen load could be dispensed with. Another mere 340 lb. could be saved by deleting an anchor chain.

These reductions were insufficient to bring much improvement so the Ministry of Aircraft Production, Coastal Command and Short's met on 9 October 1941 and agreed further deletions totalling 3,270 lb. Ammunition would be cut to 5,000 rounds (1,500 lb.), some armour and engine supercharger blowers removed. Four bomb cells and a drying-room for clothing would be deleted and flooring reduced. Slinging gear would go and lilos would replace mattresses, which gave a total saving of 3,270 lb. Remaining equipment would include self-sealing fuel tanks, armour for the pilots, A.P.U.s, sound-proofing, a refrigerator and an electric cooker. What part some of this ancillary equipment would play in the Shetland story could surely not then have been envisaged.

Revised estimates of range after these weight reductions were then computed as shown in the table overleaf.

With the possibility of war in the Far East, Coastal Command now said that a range of 4,500 nautical miles (5,800 statute miles) was necessary. The Director of Naval Operations claimed that with a 4,000 lb. bomb load the range should be 4,000 miles, but that for convoy escort earlier estimates were acceptable. He

Gross weight (lb.)	Bomb load (lb.)	Range (Statute miles)	Speed (m.p.h.)
110,000	4,000	2,700	150
120,000	4,000	3,500	150

suggested removal of the remaining dorsal turret, and said that it should still be possible to fit one if needed.

In view of the many changes being made, a completely revised specification for the aircraft was drawn up. The cruising speed would now be not less than 220 m.p.h. in weak mixture, range 1,500 miles in weak mixture when carrying full reconnaissance load and 4,000 lb. of bombs—which should be possible at an all-up weight of 120,000 lb. The aircraft needed to be able to take off in not more than 30 sec. and land within 1,000 yd. It must be able to maintain height with one engine out of use in level flight between sea level and 10,000 ft. It must be able to manoeuvre on water in a wind speed of up to 40 knots. Each of the three turrets would carry ·50 in. guns. Accommodation should be provided for 8,000 lb., 4,000 lb., 1,900 lb., 1,000 lb. and 500 lb. bombs and mines of 1,500 lb. or 2,000 lb. There would be three pilots, an air observer, fitter/air gunner, flight mechanic/air gunner, flight rigger/air gunner, wireless operator, engineer/air gunner and two radio operators/air gunners making a crew of eleven. Power would be from four Bristol Centaurus III engines. An all-up weight of 120,000 lb. would include the following items: power units 18,350 lb., tankage 3,400 lb., structure 39,400 lb., fuel 41,610 lb., crew 2,000 lb., equipment 15,230 lb. The aircraft would now have a drying-room, curtains, four officers' bunks, six crew bunks, drinking and washing water (25 gallons), two auxiliary power units, G.E.C. cooker, refrigerator, crockery rack, sink and draining board, mooring ladder, bilge pump, boat hook, awnings and covers, 'J' Type dinghies, fire axes, anchor stowage and lead for 20 fathoms.

Subsequent to the October 1941 meeting held to discuss reduced military loading a new weight analysis was drawn up at Short's. Increased weight of 1,100 lb. had arisen within the power-plant installation, although the firm had already decided to remove armour from the outer engines without admitting this. Armour weight saved at this meeting was 200 lb., not the expected 500 lb. The firm's estimate of structure weight, now agreed with R.D.T., was 38,500 lb., but R.D.T. still considered the Shetland could take off and operate at 5,000 feet if the weight did not exceed 125,000 lb. If the remaining dorsal turret was deleted, a range of 4,000 miles with a 4,000 lb. bomb load could be achieved at 125,000 lb., but if the turret was retained this would fall to 3,650 miles. By reducing the fire-depression angle of that turret and sinking it deeper in the hull useful drag reduction could be achieved.

Constant changes in load, and problems of rising weight, still worried Air Commodore J. D. Breakey. On 23 November 1941 he wrote to Air Vice-Marshal

R. S. Sorley: 'I'm doubtful of the success of 14/40, are we wise to go on with it? I'm afraid it's partly our fault this flying-boat had a bad start. We allowed C-in-C Coastal Command to place too much stress on high cruising speed. Even so, it's only about 22 m.p.h. higher than if we had gone for a long-range lightly wing-loaded aircraft such as the Americans favour.'

The Sunderland had tipped the scales some 4,000 to 5,000 lb. heavier than expected and the Stirling about 10,000 lb. above its expected loaded weight. The Stirling's performance was much below the expectations of the Air Staff. Was history to be repeated? 'Estimates for 14/40', wrote Air Commodore Breakey, 'do not meet our requirements, and I think it can never give us what we want. It is quite preposterous that we should at this stage be asked to substitute lilos for proper mattresses to save a few pounds in a flying-boat of 120,000 lb. If it is still a firm requirement that this flying-boat carries 4,000 lb. for 4,000 miles it is quite obvious the design must be reconsidered before further steps are taken.'

'Having eliminated quite a lot of weight,' Air Vice-Marshal R. S. Sorley wrote to Air Marshal F. J. Linnell, 'we have now concluded that the aircraft will work at 120,000 lb. for a 4,000-mile range, after deleting both mid-upper turrets. This leaves very little margin for increase of weight after the boat has entered service. I would like to know if it is now possible to increase the span and reduce wing-loading to achieve more economic cruise.'

In his reply the A.C.A.S.(T), Air Marshal F. J. Linnell, wrote on 16 December 1941 that he was now satisfied with 14/40, and that it would achieve 4,000 miles (land) at most economic cruise speed. R.14/40, he thought, would have a good load capacity with an all-up weight of 120,000 lb., at ranges of up to 3,000 statute miles. But Ralph Sorley's desire for a 4,000 lb. load for 4,000 miles would not be met, and it was therefore agreed to accept 4,000 lb. load for a 3,600 mile range. 'I think we would be unwise to drop it,' wrote Linnell, 'for it is our only string for the future.' So, the R.14/40, now known as the Short Shetland, went ahead at 120,000 lb. all-up weight with a 4,000 lb. load for 3,600 miles—and no dorsal turrets. Hand-held beam guns would have to suffice.

While argument raged over the Shetland's performance, what of the Blackburn R.13/40? That specification, it will be recalled, had also originated in July 1940 and called for maximum economic cruise performance at 5,000 ft. coupled with a range of 1,500 miles. Overloaded it should have a range of 3,500 miles at not less than 210 m.p.h. at 5,000 ft. It would have two ·303 in. nose guns, two ·303 in. guns in a retractable mid-upper turret and four ·303 in. guns in the tail turret. Its bomb load would be 2,000 lb. At the preliminary design conference on 28 September 1940 a maximum overloaded weight was agreed as not to exceed 52,000 lb. Range would be 3,000 land miles at 170 m.p.h. at 5,000 ft. without a bomb load, or 400 miles less with 2,000 lb. bomb load. It was at this time tentatively agreed to forgo the nose turret.

Design work went ahead then, on 4 January 1941, the specification was revised prior to a mock-up conference on 10 January. A 20 mm. cannon with sixty rounds would be sited in a power-operated nose mounting, useful for head-on attack against shipping and U-boats. The mid-upper turret would no longer be retractable, and there would be two ·303 in. beam guns on each side of the fuselage amidships. Loads of 4 × 450 lb. or 8 × 300 lb. depth charges or 4 × 1,000 lb. bombs must now be carried. These amendments were agreed on 7 February 1941. Fuel was to be carried for a still air range of 2,750 miles at 5,000 ft. at most economic cruise speed. The hoped for range of 3,500 miles was not now possible, but 2,500 nautical miles with 2,000 lb. of bombs or 3,000 miles' reinforcement range were agreed essential.

A likely comparison with the Sunderland was drawn up, as shown in the following table.

	Sunderland	*Blackburn R.13/40*
Maximum operating weight (lb.)	54/55,000	52,500
Wing area (sq. ft.)	1,700	1,400
Span	112 ft. 8 in.	98 ft.
Engine take-off power (h.p.)	4 Pegasus: 1,010/1,050	2 Centaurus: 2,050
Top speed (m.p.h.)	205/210	240/250
Economic cruise speed (m.p.h.)	130/140	165
Range with 2,000 lb. bombs (miles)	2,000	2,300
Nose guns	2 × ·303 in.	1 × 20 mm.
Mid guns	2 × ·303 in. hand-held	2 × ·50 in. in turret, 4 × ·303 in. hand-held
Tail guns	4 × ·303 in.	2 × ·50 in.

The R.13/40 would not be expected to serve beyond the demands placed upon the Sunderland. It would be faster, cruise better and have a similar range. The hull would include better layout with less wastage, and the wing area would be more generous. The Sunderland suffered from a very deep hull which induced high drag. By utilizing the retractable-pontoon hull on the R.13/40, hull drag would be reduced by 25 per cent. By comparison the larger R.14/40 Shetland would take one and a half times the man-hours to build and use twice as much fuel.

Great hopes were pinned upon the R.13/40, but by the autumn of 1941 it was in trouble. Blackburn's could not offer anything like the range now being required from the design. Its estimated operational weight had risen to 60,000 lb., which suggested a cruising speed of 154 m.p.h. The equipped weight of the aircraft was about 40,400 lb. Air Ministry representatives visited Dumbarton in November 1941 to check structure and equipment weights now that this flying-boat, too, was well over the projected weight. A 16,000 lb. structure weight had been based upon calculations relating to the earlier R.1/36, and Blackburn's now said that the structure weight could not be reduced below 18,000 lb.

The main problem with the R.13/40 was that, as it was only a twin-engined boat, provision had to be allowed for one-engine flying. The 60,000 lb. all-up weight might have been acceptable with two engines running but with one engine out of use the loaded weight, it was agreed, could not be greater than 44,500 lb., which implied a fuel load of only 4,100 lb. and a reduced range. A fundamental trouble was that the wing span was too short. If the span could have been increased to 106 feet, then the permissible weight for single-engined flying would have risen to 48,000 lb. and the safe distance from shore would have been 900 miles instead of the 500-mile maximum under existing planning.

Coastal Command's Commander-in-Chief emphasized how useful a flying-boat of the size of R.13/40 would be if it had a better performance than the Sunderland. On the other hand the Air Staff needed a range of 2,500 sea miles (2,880 land miles) with a 2,000 lb. bomb load and 3,000 miles without bombs. The only way in which these figures could have been obtained was by increasing the wing span or by deleting an essential turret. Despite higher structure weight such an aircraft would have 200 miles' increased range. One thing was not apparent: a retracting planing area gave a good return only with a smaller flying-boat and would make little appreciable difference with one the size of R.13/40. In December 1941 the Air Staff stated that even a range of 3,050 land miles without bombs was unacceptable. The R.13/40's single-engined performance grew worse as the design progressed. Originally it was speed that had made it attractive rather than the very long range now required. The Air Staff could no longer see any need for high-performance small flying-boats, and compared with the new Sunderland Mk. III, R.13/40 showed little advantage. Range was now the paramount requirement, and landplanes were in view with ranges of 2,500–3,000 miles. Accordingly, the Air Staff asked for R.13/40 to be cancelled.

On 17 December 1941 the whole project was discussed with Robert Blackburn who pointed out that increased load had raised the all-up weight so that the range required could no longer be obtained. Single-engined performance was unacceptable and Blackburn's were told on 6 January 1942 that the design was cancelled. Blackburn maintained that the retractable pontoon did improve performance even with his larger design, and wondered whether a larger boat could be designed to make use of the large amount of research work undertaken. This might have come about had not the Sunderland been suitable for development and the Shetland been to hand. That machine would now become the only new flying-boat design to be built in Britain during the war. So, after much discussion, there would no longer be a Sunderland replacement. Instead, that worthy design would be updated to outlive any other type of British flying-boat design.

Although Saunders-Roe had received no orders for any of their flying-boats they continued to produce design studies. By 1942 the much-changed operational requirements, together with the installation of new equipment, had pushed the overload weight of existing flying-boats to their limiting values, resulting in restrictions in their use. The Saro S.42 proposal submitted to the Air Ministry in July 1942 was devised to utilize the wing and power units of the Lancaster bomber wedded to the hull of the S.40 which had already been evaluated using the S.37 'Shrimp'. Based on this information a four-engined flying-boat of 55,000 lb. was designed which had a top speed of 250 m.p.h. at 9,000 ft.

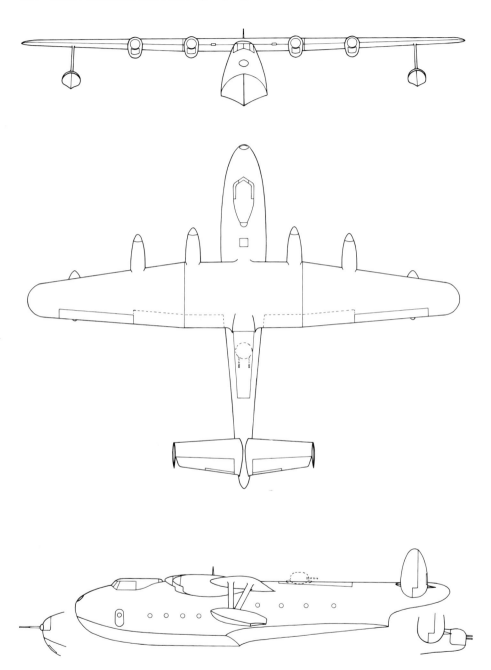

20.   Saro S.42A Freighter/Patrol flying-boat of August 1942
incorporating Lancaster bomber components

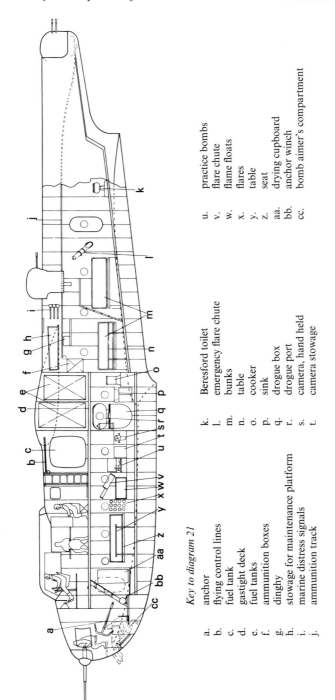

Key to diagram 21

a.	anchor
b.	flying control lines
c.	fuel tank
d.	gastight deck
e.	fuel tanks
f.	ammunition boxes
g.	dinghy
h.	stowage for maintenance platform
i.	marine distress signals
j.	ammunition track
k.	Beresford toilet
l.	emergency flare chute
m.	bunks
n.	table
o.	cooker
p.	sink
q.	drogue box
r.	drogue port
s.	camera, hand held
t.	camera stowage
u.	practice bombs
v.	flare chute
w.	flame floats
x.	flares
y.	table
z.	seat
aa.	drying cupboard
bb.	anchor winch
cc.	bomb aimer's compartment

21.   Cut-away of the Saro 42 patrol variant. Internal arrangement Saro S.42 as laid out in August 1942

Overloaded to 70,000 lb. its range would have been 3,750 miles. Thus it approximated the S.38 submitted in 1939 to R.5/39, but offered a shorter development time due to the use of tried components. The S.42A was a freight version designed to carry 35,800 lb. of cargo at the overload weight of 70,000 lb. A top speed of 240 m.p.h. at 12,000 ft. was forecast, and if the engines were changed from Merlin XX to Hercules VI a speed of 260 m.p.h. at 16,000 ft. seemed feasible. Nothing came of these projects, for favour was already veering towards landplane transports and in particular the Avro York.

During 1942 design work on the Shetland proceeded steadily. Thoughts that the aircraft could serve as a strategic bomber quietly vanished, particularly when the Shetland's mainplane was chosen to form the basis for Short's B.8/41 'Super Stirling', though later abandoned. Saunders-Roe, having lost an order for their R.14/40, and because the Shetland was the largest aircraft project yet attempted in Britain, now collaborated in its design and production. They undertook wing and engine-installation design, leaving the rest to Short's who would assemble the boats and test-fly them.

A wing section of Modified Göttingen 436 was chosen for the Shetland, Handley-Page flaps replacing the usual Gouge flaps featured by Short's boats. A very striking sweepback of the leading edge characterized the mainplane. Cells in the inner wing sections could carry mines or 4,000 lb. of bombs, and long-range tankage would be placed centrally in the hull athwart the c.g. point.

The twenty-foot-high hull posed design and production problems. Great care had to be taken in placing the hull step accurately. Should there be an error—as had happened with the Sunderland—the engine nacelles would need to be lengthened to compensate. It was considered that water tank tests would not provide accurate information, so the Saro 'Shrimp' was modified to incorporate a 4/11 scale-model of the Shetland planing surfaces and step. It underwent taxiing trials at M.A.E.E., Helensburgh, particularly to assess the effects of slipstream on the spray pattern. Various step designs were explored, a streamlined variant never providing such a steady result as the wedge step of earlier Short designs.

Short's had experience of sub-contracting for the Stirling bomber and the Shetland's hull had to be composed of sections small enough to be easily sub-contracted and moved by road. The hull was therefore designed in five lower and four upper sections, with the tail cone forming one other section. Construction of the hull followed standard Short practice being mainly of unbroken frames with interrupted stringers cleated to them. Joints between hull sections were riveted or bolted back to back. Butt straps recessed into the joggles in the skin closed the external joint lines.

Considerable and positive power was needed for the turrets to function and, for the first time in a British aircraft, a 110-volt AC electrical system was chosen.

Mainplane design was quite different from that of previous Short aircraft. Machined fittings were eliminated as far as possible, and maximum stiffness was built in to prevent bending and torsion because of the heavy loading in the wings. Fuel tanks in the mainplane held 2,928 gallons and between the outer tanks and

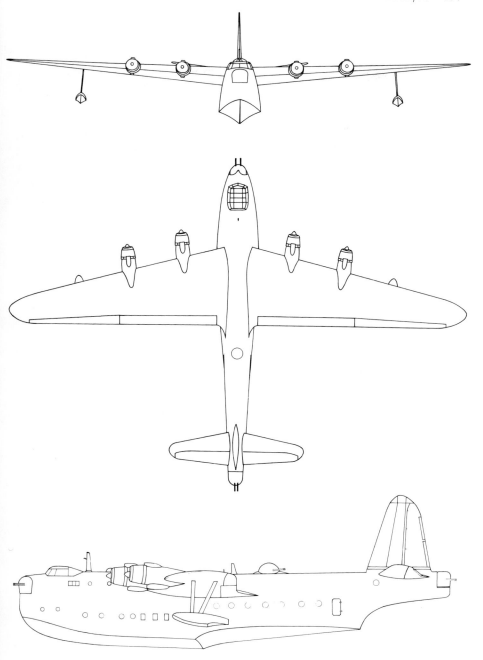

22.   General arrangement of the Short Shetland for reconnaissance duty, 1942

that in the wing root were sited six weapons' bays in each mainplane, similar in design to those of the Stirling. Loads totalling 2,000 lb. could be carried in each set of wing cells.

Bristol Centaurus VII fourteen-cylinder two-row radial engines chosen for the prototype had oil coolers slung beneath them, fed by oil tanks sited in the box spar. Dunlop de-icing equipment was installed along the wing and tailplane leading edges. Massive high-tensile steel booms across the top of the hull carried the wing torsion box built into the main frames of the hull. Between the quarter chord and auxiliary spars was sited a long-range fuel tank for 2,115 gallons coupled to a 566-gallon forward tank. For electrical power, reliance was placed upon two 60 h.p. Rotol petrol-driven auxiliary-power generators placed side by side in a compartment on the lower forward deck, and this item of equipment was to play a sombre part in the Shetland story. Above this compartment was the flight deck for a crew of five with two rest bunks. The pilots sat side by side beneath a canopy similar in shape to that of the Stirling.

The huge FN 66 gun turret was to be placed in the nose, with mooring compartment and bomb aimer's position below. Amidships was the FN 36 turret mounting four ·50 in. guns, and in the tail an FN 59 also with four ·50 in. guns and electrically powered. Internal layout was on two decks and, as with the Sunderland, was extremely spacious. The hope was that the FN 36 dorsal turret would be replaced by a twin 20 mm. Bristol B 17 turret with a B 12 to be sited here with twin ·50 in. guns and lower drag than the FN turret if the B 17 was long delayed. Supplementing the dorsal turret were single ·50 in. guns in either side of the hull. Construction of the giant machine commenced in 1943.

By this time the main particulars of the aircraft were fully established. It would be powered by four Centaurus VIISM each giving 2,525 b.h.p. at 2,500 ft., 2,030 b.h.p. at 13,250 ft. The wing span of 150 ft. made it by far the largest aircraft built in Britain so far. It had a length of 110 ft. and a maximum beam of 12 ft. 6 in. Its height above the water was 29 ft., draught 5 ft. Forecast maximum all-up weight remained at 125,000 lb. It retained provision for an internal weapon load of 24,000 lb., almost twice that of any British bomber. The ranges finally forecast are shown in the following table.

	Land miles	*Sea miles*	*Associated bomb load*
Permanent tanks full	1,470	1,280	24,000 lb.
	2,910	2,530	4,000 lb.
Auxiliary tanks full	3,620	3,145	nil

They were below those originally demanded. Cruising speeds of 252 m.p.h at 2,500 ft. and 259 m.p.h. at 13,200 ft. were forecast with most economical cruising speed of 175 m.p.h. at 5,000 ft. Such were the figures of May 1943 when a turning-point came in the career of the aircraft.

24.   Afloat at Rochester in summer 1945, DX166, the Shetland prototype

It was at this time that two major aspects of the Shetland programme had to be decided upon, production and employment. It was estimated that production would commence at the rate of one aircraft per month in July 1944, but soon the date was put back to December 1944. Final erection would take place at Short's Windermere factory. It was proposed to concentrate Stirling production at Belfast with Rochester works contributing to the programme. Swindon works would be released to build Lancasters. Blackburn's at Dumbarton would continue building Sunderlands at the rate of about eight a month and take on the Mk. IV with Rochester, where about fourteen Sunderlands would be built per month when the Stirling was phased out. Belfast works would gradually switch to Shetland production, which by October 1945 could reach about three a month rising by one from March 1946. As regards employment for the aircraft, three roles were discussed in May 1943: (a) open-sea reconnaissance, trade protection and mine laying; (b) military transport; and (c) civil transport for B.O.A.C. The last two ideas were quite new and came to eclipse the former.

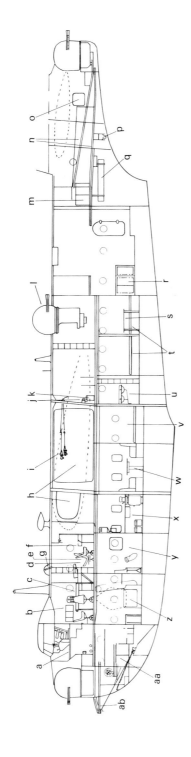

Short Shetland G.R.Mk. I – internal layout of July 1942.

Key to diagram 23

a. Flight deck with stairway to navigator's compartment
b. Navigator's compartment, table on starboard side of aircraft
c. Navigator's position
d. A.S.V radar operator's position
e. Wireless operator's position alongside A.S.V. operator
f. Flight engineer's position
g. Gunnery fire controller's position
h. Fuel tanks
i. Bomb door motors
j. Flap motor
k. Water tank
l. Dorsal turret
m. Ammunition boxes
n. Ammunition ducts (top), floor below
o. Escape hatch
p. Working position for vertical camera

q. M.D.S. coil
r. Work bench, stowage for inboard motor for the inflatable boat stowed along the port side of the compartment; rear entrance to hull on starboard side
s. Folding table
t. Compartment with four bunks, with lockers beneath each
u. Washplace and toilet
v. Officers' accommodation – two bunks
w. Officers' Mess compartment with table, clothing cupboard and rest alcove
x. Gallery with food cupboard, refrigerator, electric cooker, sink unit, electric-kettle point
y. Pyrotechnics compartment, for flares, flame floats, markers, and flare chute
z. Auxiliary generating plant, with two generators and stairway to the left
aa. Mooring compartment
ab. Anchor hoisting beam and traveller

Drawing based upon Short Bros. diagram 0357026 originally drawn up 11 December 1941 and updated 23 July 1942

23. Cut-away of the Short R.14/40 Shetland

The Short Shetland as a transport

Availability of a new military flying-boat was seen by the Air Staff as ensuring that they would not be dependent upon American sources for flying-boats once the Sunderland was withdrawn. Although the Shetland could carry 12,000 lb. of mines for short distances and thereby be a very useful minelayer, production would be so slow that no squadron would be able to form for years. Production could not be increased, because of lack of labour and the structural space needed to build these large machines. Maintenance was seen to be an immense task. Only one or two bases in the world would have facilities to maintain the aircraft thus restricting its strategic value. Manpower to operate one squadron would be considerable too. Such deliberations gave more credence to questions about the wisdom of ever embarking upon such an ambitious programme.

It looked likely that the war in Europe would finish before any aircraft became available, freeing the Shetland for civil purposes, which could include the resumption of Empire and trans-Atlantic routes. It could provide a high level of comfort and carry sizeable loads of freight and mail. Yet it would be a slow competitor to landplanes. Any redesign would require substantial structural alteration if passengers were to be carried in comfort. Production would be set back and American competitors would be in the field first. One simple conversion was credible though.

To make the Shetland suitable as a military transport structural changes would be far less radical. It would be able to carry a useful load of 10,000–15,000 lb. and could serve very usefully, supplying forces in the Far East where landplane facilities were less well developed. The total number of Shetlands needed would remain small—fitting in readily with production plans. Unfortunately, the aircraft had been planned so that most of the useful load was carried in the mainplanes. Major structural modifications would be needed if the boat were to carry in the fuselage the total possible weight of payload. Loading hatches would be needed. It was estimated that it would take an additional twelve to eighteen months to adapt it for a military-transport role. For this reason it was not a very attractive proposition, except as a freighter on Far East runs. Similarly, it was unattractive as a civil transport because it would be outdated by the time it became available. In the hands of R.A.F. Transport Command it could reach territories where landplanes could not yet land.

Thus, from May 1943 onwards, it became advisable to look upon the Shetland as a military transport, and its primary offensive role was therefore abandoned. It joined that mixed line of very large British aircraft which, for one reason or another, always seem to have been abandoned in mid-stream.

There was no simple solution to production problems. More might be built at Rochester, but this would be expensive for new buildings would be needed, and increasing the labour force there was not easy. Labour was available at Belfast, but the works there were considered more prone to strikes. Short's were likely to complain if production was too much divorced from the parent works. Clearly, production would raise many problems. Estimates suggested that about 190,000 man-hours were needed to produce a Shetland, and that about only 9,000 man-hours would be saved by building it as a transport. Conversion to civil transport would mean deletion of all guns, turrets, armour plating, bomb gear, self-sealing tanks and generating plant—a saving of about 12,000 lbs.' weight and about 40,000 man-hours. Modification to full civil standard would mean deletion of wing bomb cells and redesign of spars and hull spar frames. One saving on the military side would be to delete all turrets on the transport which would then require only one generator. However, worries about the likely range remained. It seemed feasible that the production version would have a maximum range of about 3,300 miles flying at 137 knots and carrying a load of 10,000 lb. A good fuel reserve had to be maintained so that the effective range might be as low as 2,200 miles.

With the development of navigation aids one of the advantages of the flying-boat was fast disappearing. There really was no need now for the Shetland—other than to encourage the design of large flying-boats for post-war use, and to gain experience of them. The Shetland would be uneconomic as a military aircraft, although lack of airfields in certain countries might still limit the usefulness of landplanes. On 29 May 1943 a meeting was held at the Air Ministry to discuss possible uses for a Shetland transport. It could lift large power plants over stage lengths of 1,500 miles, carry fully equipped troops, or twenty-four day passengers and twenty by night or about twenty stretchers—all of which seemed small loads for such a large machine. Sound-proofing would be needed for passenger work. Short's had prepared for B.O.A.C. a scheme for fifty-three day or eighteen day/night passengers. Such an aircraft could serve the Shannon–Botwood route cruising at 185 m.p.h., or Shannon–New York, or Vancouver–Honolulu; but such flights would be of very long duration and passenger loads very limited. With suitable modifications the military freight load might reach 15,000 lb., but at a gross weight of 125,000 lb. it would still be more like 13,000 lb. Large landplanes would certainly offer better returns.

During June 1943 it was decided that the Shetland would go ahead, but only as a transport. Ten were still on order for the R.A.F., but where and how to produce them remained a problem. Short's now had a Stirling transport in view and, just as the fate of the Shetland had been decided, almost on the same day the Stirling had been selected for a transport future. Even by cutting the Stirling transport programme Shetland production would not be increased. Building Shetlands might even prevent the Belfast works producing the more important Lancaster IV, which was being planned in the face of opposition from Short's. Production of the Shetland could be put back to 1946, and another possibility was to halt Sunderland production at Belfast, but Sunderlands would be needed for the foreseeable future.

Meanwhile, the building of the first prototype, DX166, proceeded at

25. Great skill and a love of aeroplanes combined to raise Charles Brown to the top
level of aviation photographers. His photograph here shows the Shetland to advantage

26.   One might regard the Shetland as a combination of features of two Short forerunners, the Sunderland and the Stirling

27.   The sharp sweep-back of the mainplanes of the Shetland can be seen here. The Shetland can also be seen to have been a very large aeroplane

28. There's no doubt about it, a Short flying-boat was a breathtaking sight

Rochester—the second aircraft, DX171, having also been started. By the end of 1943 it was certain that only the first example would be completed for military use and, now that turrets had been deleted, the crew was reduced to ten. Plans for the S.35 Civil Conversion were in hand now. It would have a streamlined nose and tail and absence of bomb doors would bring a combined reduction of 19,000 lb. The civil aircraft would not have self-sealing fuel tanks, but modifications to the aircraft added 3,800 lb. weight after turrets, etc., had been deleted. The R.A.F. transport had 2,000 lb. added to permit carriage of heavy loads, and the civil version showed a fuel-consumption saving owing to better streamlining.

In February 1944 the hull of the prototype was moved on to hard-standing outside the works at Rochester. By May the machine had been largely assembled, the wings having come by land from Saro. The mass of scaffolding around the prototype was removed in July 1944; then three months for engine and systems testing were followed by fitting out, before DX166 was launched on to the River Medway on 24 October 1944.

While the prototype was being built the little Saro A.37 'Shrimp' had been giving good service as a test-bed for the Shetland. Comparison of the model with the full-scale machine showed the characteristics set out in the following table.

Item	Saro A.37	Saro scaled-up to Shetland	Shetland actual
Wing:			
area (sq. ft.)	340	2,570	2,624
span (ft.)	50	137·5	150·3
standard mean chord (ft.)	6·8	18·7	17·46
aspect ratio	7·35	7·35	8·6
angle to keel	4·39°	4·39°	4°
section	NACA 20316 to NACA 4409 at tip	—	Got. Mod. 436
lift	6° 9′	6° 9′	6° 12′
weight as tested (lb.)	5,600	117,000	—

Following hull trials a scaled-down Shetland fin and rudder were fitted and in April 1944 trials of the Shetland-type wing-tip floats and elevators were undertaken over the speed range 60–110 knots. The machine was very stable which boded well for the full-sized aircraft. Shetland-type floats had been earlier fitted and tests continued at wind speeds up to 28 m.p.h. and in cross winds and down winds at 5,700 lb. all-up weight. Careful siting of the floats would, it was deduced, reduce the spray. There followed tests with a scale Shetland hull bottom, wing-tip floats and tail combined, indicating that the Shetland would be stable at 120,000 lb. Porpoising might occur at the hump at very high loading. A twin-tail arrangement, such as the A.37 previously had, would now have been

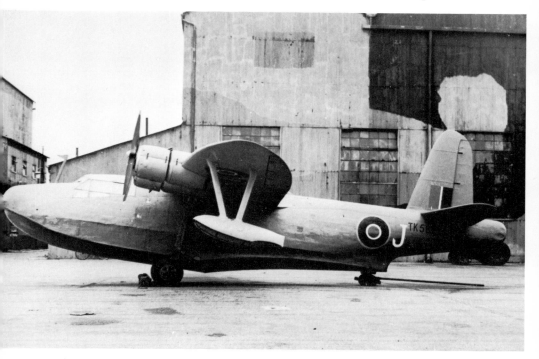

29. The Saro 37 with Shetland-style tail unit. Its finish was Dark Slate Grey and Extra Dark Sea Grey with yellow undersurfaces. 'J' appeared in white on the rear fuselage alongside the serial number TK580 which was also applied beneath the mainplanes

advantageous. Some porpoising might occur in a lightly loaded Shetland on landing, but it would not be serious.

Tension rose at Rochester as the giant boat was prepared for flight trials. Then—on 14 December 1944—John Lankester Parker, with Geoffrey Tyson, took off from the Medway and made a thirty-minute flight at 85,000 lb. There could be no denying that the Shetland was a majestic sight. By 1 January 1945 three flights had been made and in mid-January the prototype was at Windermere for weighing and c.g. determination. However, the necessary 15-foot diameter propellers did not become available until late March 1945.

Early flight trails were without major incident, the aircraft performing well, so much so that there was soon a suggestion for ordering a dozen of the civil version. Then, on 5 March 1945, R.A.F. Transport Command notified that they would like to operate six Shetlands. By late March so attractive did the aircraft seem that there was talk of using the ten on order to promote a post-war Shetland programme. Such hopes were abruptly squashed when, on 9 April 1945, it was stated that the Shetland was no longer needed for the R.A.F. Furthermore, it was revealed that there was no firm official civil requirement in mind. The six that

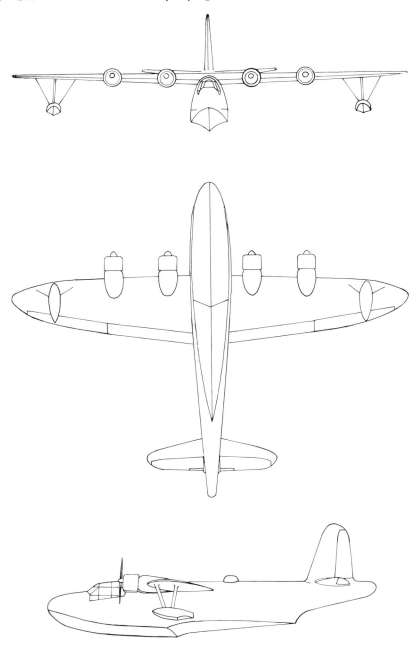

24.   Saro 37 revised to incorporate Shetland features,
layout of September 1942. Length 41.5 ft., height 15.25 ft.

30.   The first Shetland, flaps down, approaches the Medway for landing

Transport Command would like could only be acquired over a number of years, for the aircraft had become far too expensive for the R.A.F. They were only prepared to operate them if financed by the Ministry of Aircraft Production and for development purposes. B.O.A.C. took a similar point of view—they would operate them but funding would have to come from M.A.P. The cost of the two prototypes was about £300,000 each and if six more were built each would cost about £150,000—a total of £900,000 which was very considerable at that time. If the order for six for Transport Command was to go ahead it would have to be at the expense of several new fighters or the new heavy bomber programme. Post-war funding would be very strictly controlled.

By July 1945 it was clear that the R.A.F. did not need Shetland transports, which would absorb much of one whole year's funding for new aircraft. Even if M.A.P. funded them, it seemed of doubtful value for the R.A.F. to operate them. They would provide only limited data for they would soon be outdated since they did not have turbo-prop engines. The two prototypes would provide enough data on large flying-boats. Air Commodore J. N. Boothman considered there was little likelihood that six Shetlands could provide much useful data to assist in the development of the 300,000 lb. long-range flying-boat that Blackburn's and Saro were now jointly exploring. Rather more important, it was now obvious that the question was arising of whether the R.A.F. had any need for flying-boats. Large, long-range landplanes and suitable airfields for them were becoming available fast. If the flying-boat's application was for commercial purposes only why should the R.A.F. shoulder the cost? For R.A.F. purposes there might be a small flying-boat. What, the Air Staff asked, does a large flying-boat offer that a small one does not? Clearly, the flying-boat was in decline. In July 1945 the idea of six Shetlands was firmly dropped. The only examples now would be the two prototypes.

An interesting interjection came at this time. Air Marshall Sir Douglas C. S. Evill, Vice-Chief of the Air Staff, pointed out that since flying-boats did not need elaborate bases they might in future be very useful as strategic bombers. Jet-propelled and of refined form, they would operate from bases without vulnerable runways—an idea which still makes sense. Nothing came of his suggestion.

Saunders-Roe had meanwhile been considering the future for flying-boats and remained convinced that they had a major part to play in the post-war scene. In September 1944 an Outline Proposal for a four-engined flying-boat had been put forward by the Design Project Office at Beaumaris. This included a most radical new concept, for it featured Rolls-Royce Merlin XX engines to work in coupled pairs and be completely buried in the wing structure. Such a layout was to be adopted by the company for the Princess flying-boat. The 1944 design was much smaller than the Princess, with an all-up weight of 55,000 lb., a maximum speed of 275 m.p.h. at 20,500 ft. and a range of 3,000 miles. Thus it fell into the category of a Sunderland replacement. But the very success of the Sunderland, and the possibility of a Mk. IV ideally serving the R.A.F., after the war, brought about rejection of the idea. Even more significant for the future were two other Saunders-Roe Outline Proposals of September 1944. The first was for a six-engined long-range transport flying-boat intended to make direct flights between London and New York. It had an all-up weight of 187,000 lb., maximum speed of 317 m.p.h. at 14,000 ft. and a range of 3,600 miles. For their design study Saro utilized data earlier obtained from that very valuable little aeroplane the S.37.

As a companion to this second project there was another which took the concept of buried coupled engines a stage further. It was for an eight-engined long-range flying-boat transport fitted with coupled Bristol Centaurus engines. With an all-up weight of 250,000 lb.—double that of the Shetland—its forecast maximum speed was 331 m.p.h. at 14,000 ft., range 3,600 miles. Payload would have been 21,700 lb. compared with 13,150 lb. of the six-engined proposal. Such a large flying-boat would have to await the post-war scene before emerging as the stupendous and breathtaking Princess. From the accompanying general-arrangement drawings the part played by designs stemming from R.5/39 in the ultimate configuration of the Princess are gradually apparent. Despite the rejection of R.5/39 it was the key specification to wartime and indeed post-war British military flying-boat design.

As the war against Japan ended, the second prototype was being built as a civil aircraft and was about 60 per cent complete. Short's were rapidly running low on work and with this in mind the Air Staff carried out an evaluation of the wartime use of flying-boats.

They had mainly served in a general reconnaissance role, but also for air/sea rescue, transport and for evacuation purposes. Preference for landplanes by Coastal Command in the later stages of the war mainly arose because of the absence of flying-boat bases in the United Kingdom. Landplanes had, statistically, proved more efficient, but in certain parts of the world flying-boats were useful when they could perform where landplanes could not. They could operate from unprepared bases or in conjunction with depot ships, and needed little more than a safe anchorage. One might see, here, a similarity between such operation and that of today's Harriers. But in the western hemisphere it was difficult to foresee now a situation when suitable landplane bases did not exist, and since the airfields existed it would be imprudent not to use them. It was different in South-East Asia and the Pacific areas where such bases were still few. Flying-boats would need to be with mobile units, and operate from a depot. As a strategic bomber the landplane was superior.

Arising from this survey was the recommendation that flying-boats should be kept for long-range general-reconnaissance operations and for transport duties beyond the scope of landplanes. This meant an on-station patrol range of 1,000 miles over 24 hours at 200 knots' cruise with a top speed not less than 250 knots. The flying-boat should carry weapons sufficient for four attacks and an 8,000 lb. offensive load, and have reasonable defence capability against fighter attack. It should have accommodation for two crews, be easy to maintain from advanced bases and have a take-off run to unstick of not over 2,000 yd. It should not exceed 150,000 lb. all-up weight and operate between sea level and 20,000 ft. In a transport role its maximum range would be 5,500 miles, minimum 2,500 miles in still air, and it would cruise at heights up to 30,000 ft. Such a machine would need to be powered by gas turbine engines.

31.   Shetland DX166 cruises over the River Medway

The Shetland was certainly not the flying-boat to meet these requirements but a possibility to be considered was a combined development of the Sunderland and the Shetland. It was estimated that the Shetland could be loaded to 135,000 lb. but certainly no more. Its range with 4,000 lb. load might extend to 3,900 miles if armament could be replaced by 20 mm. guns in barbettes. But even with increased span and hull refinement it was doubtful whether it could achieve 4,300 miles and cruise at over 183 m.p.h. (159 knots). The latest development of the Sunderland was by this time the Short Seaford at 75,000 lb., whose weight might be able to increase to 85,000 lb. which would certainly mark the ultimate development of the Sunderland.

On 31 August 1945 the Chief of the Air Staff suggested that the M.A.P. proceed along two lines, and place a new flying-boat in the next year's programme, where it became specified as the R.36/46. The size would have to be kept down and range extension could be achieved by in-flight refuelling. Money seemed unlikely to be available for a large military flying-boat, but one might be funded with some cost carried by civilian operators. It was presently estimated that it would be six years before a new flying-boat would emerge. The question was whether to persevere with the Shetland or continue only with the Sunderland. The former had the advantage of two crews, which cut fatigue. No conclusion was reached at this time but at a meeting on the same day it was agreed that the smallest general-reconnaissance flying-boat likely to emerge would be as large as the Shetland—suggesting that there was some advantage in persevering with it, if only to gain experience.

Again, Air Commodore J. N. Boothman came out against the Shetland explaining that the nation would not get £900,000-worth of value from six Shetlands. New weapons were now needed and the Shetland was not designed to carry these. The Shetland was little more than a scaled-up Sunderland and he felt that a lot of fuss had been made about an aircraft twice its size. 'No one', he pointed out, 'seems very concerned—nor should they—at the jump from the Tudor to the Brabazon. The Shetland is very old-fashioned, out of date. Two prototypes in being are now transports because, two years ago, no other use could be found for the Shetland.' On 12 December 1945 it was finally decided not to buy any more Shetlands for the R.A.F.

What of the progress of the prototype? In the closing weeks of the war a team from M.A.E.E. had arrived at Rochester to conduct preliminary handling of DX166 progressively at 93,000 lb., 105,000 lb. and 117,000 lb. Stability on the water they found to be good, spray characteristics normal. General manoeuvrability was as good as the Sunderland's, which was excellent. Take off and landing were normal except just after landing off the hump when a wing tended to drop and a float dig in. Lighter ailerons might avoid this. Elevator control was satisfactory over the whole speed range, but ailerons were heavy due to some friction. The aircraft was longitudinally stable under all flight conditions. It was generally pleasant to fly. There was nothing to complain about as regards handling, but the machine was certainly slow for the period.

During August 1945 it was stripped of its grey–green–yellow paintwork and

32.   In the summer of 1945, DX166 was stripped of its camouflage paint to bring its appearance more in line with a post-war transport aircraft

given a silver image in keeping with new transport aircraft. In such form it was, if anything, an even more majestic sight. Never was this more true than when it roared across the Sebro works at Bourn one bright autumn afternoon to be thrown about like some gigantic fighter, to the thrill of the workforce (and uninvited me!), to whom it was being displayed. After more development flying at Rochester it was delivered to M.A.E.E. Felixstowe for full official assessment and was now powered by four Centaurus XIs which had Stromberg injection and drove D.H. Hydromatic fully-feathering four-bladed propellers.

At Felixstowe the good stability of the boat on the water was again apparent and floats proved adequate for support in wind speeds of up to 30 knots. Control harmonization between ailerons and elevators, though, had still to be achieved. In flight it was longitudinally stable. The circuit speed at 120,000 lb. was about 140–145 knots, best approach speed 120 knots and landing speed 102 knots reduced to 88 knots at 95,000 lb. Cruising speed was about 143 knots and the still air range at 120,000 lb. calculated as 3,830 sea miles at T.A.S., 159 knots at 8,000 ft., giving a duration of 25·9 hours, or 3,754 miles during 25·6 hours which was what was now expected. With 7–8° flap the machine took off after a 49·5 sec. run reaching 106 knots I.A.S. at take off at 120,000 lb. in normal conditions. At 125,000 lb. take-off run was 159 sec. after a traverse of about 2,200 yards (estimated). Speed limitations were established as 261 knots at 97,000 lb., 249 knots T.A.S. at 120,000 lb., 228 knots T.A.S. at 125,000 lb. to which weight the machine was handled.

Manoeuvrability on the water was very good despite the lack of reversible pitch propellers, and the turning circle was as small as the Sunderland's. The response to throttle movements was very rapid, useful on narrow waterways. The floats kept well clear of the water when taxiing downwind or submerged slightly, and were about three inches clear of the water at 120,000 lb. in still conditions, although a fine spray would enter the propeller disc in 15-knot wind when taxiing at 120,000 lb. All these figures were creditable and the aircraft came up to full expectations.

Flight trials showed that the best technique for take off was to check the initial rise of the nose as speed increased and ease the aircraft off on to the step by slight push on the control column, but too fine trimming had to be watched to avoid porpoising which could be checked by backward movement of the control column. Starboard swing on take off at low weights could be corrected by rudder, but at heavy weights engine settings would need changing. By pulling the control column three-quarters back from central the aircraft could take off at 102 knots at 120,000 lb. When the flaps were raised it became slightly nose heavy. Landing approach was at 120 knots to reduce the rate of sink to 1,000 f.p.m. and not more than 25° flap was used, to avoid spray damage to the flaps. Below about 102 knots the aircraft seemed likely to skip on touchdown and have a wing drop. At 116,000 lb. stalling speed was found to be 88 knots I.A.S. flaps down. Initial climb rate at 125,000 lb. was 900 f.p.m. Pilot's view ahead was good—except at mooring.

As trials proceeded two take offs were made at 125,000 lb. Full left rudder was

33.   The graceful lines of many flying-boats belied their huge size

34.   A marked feature of the Shetland was the very sharp sweep back of the wing leading edge

needed with throttle correction to swing, and take-off speed was 111 knots I.A.S. Trials were flown at 240 knots I.A.S. and care was needed not to exceed speed limitations.

Thus, all seemed to be going remarkably well. DX166 had been delivered for M.A.E.E. trials on 13 January 1946 and for two weeks an appreciable amount of flying had taken place at Felixstowe. Then, without the slightest warning, disaster struck and in an unlikely manner. DX166 was at anchorage with two Leading Aircraftmen aboard on guard duty. They had joined the flying-boat at its anchorage at 08.00 hours on 27 January 1946. At about 20.00 hours they started the port auxiliary generating plant to charge up batteries to supply power to the cooking grill and heating lamps. After about two hours the generating plant was switched off and the cooling air shutters closed.

Early the next morning one of the airmen ran the port plant because the accumulators were low and he wanted to make some cocoa. He ran it making sure the shutter was open, but the emergency lighting was poor. With the power now being supplied he then switched on the grill and went back to his rest bunk. After about ten minutes he glanced out of a port porthole and noticed sparks. He rushed forward to find the port auxiliary generating plant compartment was full of smoke. There were no flames and he opened the shutter. As he hastened forward the generating plant stopped. He opened the bow door to let out the smoke, then ran aft to awaken his colleague. Flames then burst from the compartment so he grabbed two blankets and an extinguisher which he played on the compartment. He was soon overcome by the smoke as he tried to smother the flames with a blanket. However the fire had already taken hold, so he rushed upstairs to summon help by firing a Very pistol, but there was dense smoke on the flight deck so he had to get air in the bow by opening the door.

He then tried again to reach the flight deck, and also to release a dinghy, but flames from the compartment drove him back. Flames had now engulfed the whole of the auxiliary generating plant compartment. Both men went to the aft door shouting for a dinghy. No help came, so they jumped into the Stour and swam ashore—regrettably forgetting to turn off the fuel supply. Within a few moments fire engulfed the entire aircraft and, before any flame float could reach it, the Shetland sank in twenty-four feet of water at 06.30 hours. The total flying time for DX166 amounted to ninety hours and at the time of the accident it had aboard 5,452 gallons of fuel and 288 gallons of oil which, with ballast, held the weight at 125,000 lb.

Salvage began immediately but it was some time before divers located the wreck. The fore part of the hull was raised by its mooring chain and brought ashore. The aft section was recovered later. The aircraft had burnt down to the waterline then broken into two parts. Other sections had sunk in five feet of mud and after four days salvage was abandoned. Examination of the fore part of the hull showed the auxiliary generating plants in place and both severely damaged by fire. Cooling shutters to the port plant were fully open and the master fuel cock was fully open too, being fed from the main hull tank which had contained 2,115 gallons of petrol. The discharged fire extinguisher had proven ineffective.

35. The prototype Shetland roars over the countryside, portraying good flying qualities during a steep bank

Rotol examined the auxiliary generating plant but there was no evidence of pre-fire mechanical damage. During the investigations it was learned that oil breathing had been known to occur under abnormal loads. The Court of Inquiry finally decided that the engine had been run with the air-cooling shutters closed, despite the fact that they had been found open when wreckage was examined. In October 1945, when the aircraft was at Short's, an auxiliary generating plant had once been started with the shutters closed and the unit had overheated. It was concluded that in future the auxiliary generating plant should be so designed that it could not be started with the shutters closed.

The second machine, the civil conversion, was already well advanced. Schemes in hand for its civilian use allowed for up to seventy passengers to be carried on two decks, but eventually a load of forty was decided upon. During 1946 DX171 was completed as G-AGVD, but it was 15 September 1947—just after the S.B.A.C. Show that year—that it was launched. It flew two days later. Then it was ferried from Rochester to Belfast for furnishing. It had a revised fuel system without hull tanks, the rear hull tank being replaced by the mail compartment. Aft of that, in the upper deck, were the galley and the dining saloon which was reached by way of a stairway. The Rotol generating units were sited further forward than was the case in DX166. There were twelve wing fuel tanks to carry 6,112 gallons and the inner propellers were of the reversible pitch type. Control lines to flying controls were fitted with boosters. By this time B.O.A.C. had lost all interest in the civil Shetland II, but it was continued for possible fitting of Napier Nomad compound engines to suit it for very long-range trans-ocean flying.

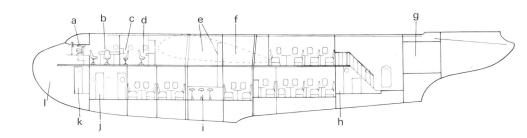

Key to diagram 25

a.	Pilot and co-pilot	e.	Galley with service lift aft	i.	Cocktail bar, seating to port
b.	Navigator	f.	Baggage compartment	j.	Toilets and washrooms
c.	Radio operator	g.	Mail (1,560 lb.)	k.	Forward entry
d.	Flight engineer	h.	Toilets	l.	Mooring compartment

25.   Interior layout of civil conversion of the Shetland for the accommodation of 53 day passengers, of May 1943

In September 1946 Short's proposed a new design loosely based upon the Shetland, the S.A.8, to be powered by four Napier Nomads. In May 1947 they updated the design to incorporate a pressurized double-bubble hull. It came too late, for civil long-range landplanes were establishing themselves. The end of the British military flying-boat was, on the other hand, some way off. Saro and Short's were working on seaplane jet fighters. Specification R.36/46 had evolved from deliberations at the end of the war only to be shelved and superseded by a new scheme.

A draft of Operational Requirement 231 appeared in November 1946. A very seaworthy, easily maintained, self-sufficient twelve-man flying-boat was needed for Indian and Pacific Ocean service. After a 1,000-mile transit, patrol station would be held for eight hours at 5,000 ft. when carrying 8,000 lb. of offensive weapons. In essence this was a set of proposals similar to those formulated at the end of the war.

It was a questionable project, yet since the Sunderland served so successfully it seemed sensible to keep a small flying-boat force. Sufficient Sunderlands remained for five more years, so it was also argued that funding should go to more urgent new aircraft while Avro Shackletons replaced some Sunderlands.

Important trade routes, however, lay beyond their range. Plans were set in motion for a flying-boat of 200,000–224,000 lb. all-up weight powered by six or eight Centaurus engines. Napier's Nomad, a compound engine with low fuel consumption, was a more attractive power plant.

Coastal Command suggested that sufficient range was obtainable from a smaller boat by employing in-flight refuelling. Only a handful of the large boats could be acquired, when many were necessary for effective submarine search. The Command wanted Very Long Range flying-boats so they stressed the in-flight refuelling idea which, for aircraft operating from remote bases, was impracticable.

Within days another expansive idea for a six-Nomad design of 175,000 lb. was being promoted. It was still far too large and its action radius of 500 miles coupled with $5\frac{1}{2}$-hour station patrol brought its early dismissal.

More suggestions continued into 1947, as the Sunderland's days looked likely to end in 1952 owing to shortage of engine spares. In June it was learnt that Short's on vacating Rochester had scrapped all Sunderland spares jigs. Anger flowed. There had been official notions of building new Sunderlands with better power plants because an entirely new design would take $6\frac{1}{2}$ years to reach service. If existing Sunderlands managed to survive for five years there would still be an eighteen-month gap before OR/231 was available.

Then the new specification was redrafted. It must serve in the Arctic as well as the tropics, use primitive slipways, and hang from a depot ship's crane, which limited all-up weight to 90,000 lb. This size held financial and operational limitations, but was realistic. Priorities attaching to it were established as (i) the anti-submarine weapons load, (ii) all-up weight, (iii) range and patrol duration, (iv) advanced maintenance simplicity and (v) speed and ceiling. It would have to reach its patrol area as fast as possible, thereby reducing crew fatigue, and remain on station at 120–170 knots.

A four-hour patrol would follow 1,000 mile transit, the weapon load being cut to 4,000 lb. A dorsal Bristol B 17 twin 20 mm. cannon turret would afford fighter defence, and twin 20 mm. attack cannon be fitted in the nose. Crew numbering seven or eight would include two pilots. Offensive loads depending upon range could be 32×250 lb. AS bombs, $8 \times 1,000$ lb. GP/MC bombs, 8 'Dealers' or $4 \times 2,000$ lb. 'Zetas' and 8 rocket projectiles. ASP 20 ASV radar with its eight-foot scanner would guide the aircraft.

Upon receiving the draft Coastal Command stated that the flying-boat would now be too small, evolving into a Long Range and not a Very Long Range aircraft. It must become larger for unlike a landplane its size was not limited by airfield and runway considerations. At 250,000/300,000 lb. a flying-boat would be 'efficient', 'economic', 'well worth the cost and effort'. The Director of Operational Requirements replied that such a machine would be far too costly, and difficult to manoeuvre. Contrary to Coastal Command's desires it could only be obtained in small numbers.

Financial stringency prohibited such a machine, and it might also bring about an inadequate aircraft. Under Plan F, R.A.F. maritime strength was for sixty-five aircraft serving in all theatres. Maximum endurance was therefore essential in any future maritime aircraft, and a sizeable crew handling submarine detection.

Coastal Command now agreed that 1,000-mile transit leading to a four-hour patrol was acceptable, and Director of Operational Requirements redrafted OR/231. It would have moderate range and last for ten years. Aircraft were costing about £2 10s per lb. weight and the new flying-boat would have an all-up weight not exceeding 100,000 lb., preferably 90,000 lb. It would be able to operate in a lowest sea temperature of 29°F., in a sea with a 4–5 ft. trough to crest. Exhaust-blown Turbo-Griffon engines were being suggested, permitting the 90,000 lb. all-up weight, whereas Nomads raised it to 105,000 lb. The increasing importance of anti-submarine effectiveness made this still the most important feature, followed now by range and endurance and a minimum speed of 200 knots when proceeding to the patrol area. Worry that the Nomad might need special fuel delayed the requirement, and it was 6 October 1948 before Specification R.2/48, the last for a British military flying-boat, was issued to the industry.

It was now that an astonishing proposition arose. Why not resurrect the Shetland? Response was immediate, and perhaps to squash the notion it was suggested that 300 knots, not even 200, was the speed needed for the positioning flight.

On receiving R.2/48, contractors were presented with a requirement for a flying-boat, of which eighty would be built. The Ministry of Supply favoured the Nomad engine despite its greater weight, questioning whether good enough performance could ever be obtained with Centaurus. A new 6-foot diameter scanner must affect the configuration, likewise the carrying of a 35-foot airborne lifeboat.

Progress on the designs was discussed on 27 January 1949 with performance being unlikely to be met by a boat of less than 110,000 lb. An updating of the

Shetland was reconsidered, for the boat was already developed but needed redesign to accommodate a larger scanner and modern weapons such as the 17-foot Pentane. A further study by Coastal Command indicated that such a machine available within two or three years would cost £349,500, or £1,000,000 less than a new design.

In June 1949 came the Design Advisory Conference. Three firms producing designs indicated first flights 3½ years hence and a revised Shetland a year away – if Nomads became available for it. But this revised Shetland was too heavy, its range too short. Under Plan F, allowance was for five flying-boat squadrons and suggestions were being made that even two of these should be replaced by Shackletons, leaving remaining Sunderlands to be available into 1955. But the Operations Staff wanted a new flying-boat, useful where airfields remained few. They maintained that the 86,000 lb. Shackleton's area of operations would be restricted by available runways. Is the Shetland totally unsuitable, they enquired?

Slow transit, slow dive to attack, radar scanner unsatisfactorily sited within the bow planing, poor flight-deck layout, nacelle-sited weapon bays—all were outdated features, and no more was to be heard of the 'new' Shetland.

Staff at Coastal Command examined the R.2/48 designs. Short's contender seemed to be an adaptation of a civil aircraft, performance having priority over all else. Vickers submitted a clean, attractive design with good development potential although its hull and flight deck were inferior to those of the first choice, the Saro P.162. That firm hade made 'a very good attempt' with an advanced hull design and well-planned flight deck. In appearance the design was handsome, in line with earlier Saro designs. Any production form would need a large freight entry door.

Before finally selecting the P.162 the Air Staff considered the only other possible contender, the Short Seaford with its all-up weight now raised to 78,000 lb. with a four-hour patrol capability after a 660-mile positioning flight. Cruising at 170 knots the Seaford could not meet the specification.

July 1949 proved the watershed time. When the Tender Review took place on 5 July 1949 the committee were reminded that the future of the British flying-boat was at stake. The 1940 Shetland could not be rejuvenated with Nomads, enter production in 1953 and serve for ten years. Such was unthinkable! Its hull hydrodynamics were quite good, but it could at best be a makeshift, operable at a weight grossly in excess of its design weight. Instead the choice was the Saro with its high length/beam ratio hull which, in conjunction with high dead rise, would give good rough water hydrodynamic performance. Against the maximum speed of 244 knots at 10,000 ft. of the Centaurus engined modified Shetland, and a lengthy cruise to the patrol area carrying a 4,000 lb. load, the P.162 with Compounded Griffons had a forecast maximum weak mixture cruising speed of 244 knots at 15,600 ft. Alternatively it cruised at 200 knots at 15,000 ft. when fitted with Turbo Griffons. With the latter engines and at 99,000 lb. all-up weight about 8.4 hours' cruise was possible when 1,000 nautical miles from base.

The Air Staff opted for the P.162. Saro forged ahead refining the aircraft and

36.   An artist's impression of the Saunders-Roe P.162 flying-boat designed to Specification R.2/48

considering various engine installations. The early 1950s were times of rapid change in aircraft design, and much that was costly to develop. In the case of the flying-boat, the Sunderland was still giving its excellent service and in 1952 work on the Saro P.162 was halted. Future long-range maritime patrol would be undertaken by landplanes after all. In 1951 the civil Shetland II had been scrapped.

That of course was not the end of the British flying-boat, for the Saro Princess story had yet to unfold. Saro soon had in hand the jet-propelled Duchess, and plans for truly gigantic flying-boats. Nothing came of any of them, except the Princess—surely one of the most impressive aircraft of all time.

Thus, it was the Shetland after all that ended that long line of beautiful flying-boats from Short's. That fire at Felixstowe where the wake of flying-boats had rippled the Stour for half a century, had been a spectacular ending to an epoch that slowly died. For the Sunderland, many years of service lay ahead and not until 20 May 1959 did that magnificent machine cease to serve the Royal Air Force.

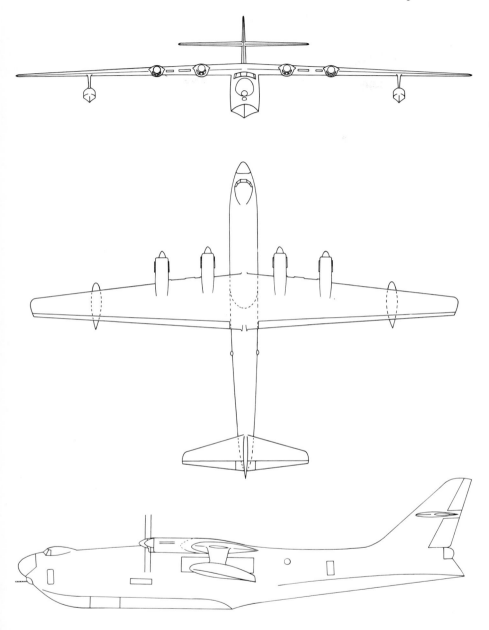

26.   The Specification R.2/48 and subsequent changes in requirements resulted in a family of
designs being produced in the period 1950–4 against the Saro P.162 design study. Final
submissions showed a single tail unit on the P.162B depicted here. The specification for this
aircraft dated April 1953 showed a projected all-up weight of 135,000 lb., power from four Napier
Nomads, crew of 14, wing span of 155 feet, length of 122.5 feet and with a flying weight of
115,000 lb. and a speed of 280 knots at 20,000 feet

By any reckoning, twenty-one years' service record is an outstanding one. The majestic Sunderland, which had undergone steady development throughout the war, served most usefully, gracefully outliving every attempt to find its replacement. Fair comment it is for sure that it was just too good to be replaced.

A Note on Sources

Recent release of official documents has provided a wealth of material adding considerably to information generally available on the origins and development of British military aircraft. The items may be consulted in the Public Record Office, Kew. The following notes suggest reference numbers of documents relating to the aircraft types with which this volume deals.

Supermarine Spitfire XII

Early development of the Griffon Spitfire is dealt with in AVIA 15/69 and AVIA 15/1055. AIR 16/691 relates to Fighter Command interest in such an aeroplane. The Spitfire XII is dealt with in a series of A. & A.E.E. Reports in set No. 692 now within the Spitfire performance reports held in AVIA 18. General policy relating to Spitfire development may be read in AIR 2/2824 and AIR 2/2825. The handbook for the Spitfire XII is available as AIR 10/2417. The aircraft's operational career may be read in the Operations Record Books for 41 Squadron (AIR 27/425 and AIR 27/426) and for 91 Squadron (AIR 27/740 and AIR 27/741). Appendices to No. 11 Group Operations Record Books are a useful source of material relating to the use of the Spitfire XII against flying-bombs, AIR 215/213 probably being the best to consult. A useful history of the Rolls-Royce Griffon engine may be found in *Flight* for 20 September 1945.

Armstrong Whitworth Albemarle

Origin of the Albemarle is outlined in AIR 2/3352 dealing with B.18/38 Type Requirements. General policy relating to the Albemarle may be found in AIR 20/3017. Performance and loading data, somewhat incomplete, are available within AVIA 18. Worry about the costing of the aircraft can be found in the Albemarle Select Committee notes. The operational career of the aircraft can be read in the respective squadron Operations Record Books, AIR 27/1644 for 295 Squadron, AIR 27/1645 for 296 Squadron, AIR 27/1648 for 297 Squadron and AIR 27/2041 for 570 Squadron. Appendices to these items give further useful material. No. 42 Operational Training Unit is dealt with in AIR 26/269. Various items concerning the Albemarle appear in AIR 29/516 and other appendices to the records of the Airborne Forces Experimental Establishments. Notes on the Heavy Glider Conversion Units may be found in AIR 29/526. Albemarle operations are also dealt with in the 38 Group Operations Record Book Appendix AIR 25/588. Among the generally published features on the Albemarle is a detailed account and cutaway drawing in *The Aeroplane* of 30 June 1944.

Short Shetland

The career of the Sunderland replacement may be researched in a variety of documents at the Public Record Office. AIR 2/2219 is concerned with schemes for the R.3/38 and R.5/39. AVIA 15/441 outlines flying-boat policy 1939–41 and AIR 20/3140 is devoted to the Shetland and AIR 20/1771 with policy particularly relating to R.14·40. AVIA 15/1740, AVIA 15/2738 and AVIA 19/610 deal with Shetland flight trials. Post-war flying-boat policy details may be found in AIR 2/5956. Copies of *The Aeroplane* for 25 May, 1 June, 27 July, 7 December 1945 and 17 March 1950 along with copies of *Flight* for 21 June 1945, 6 February 1947 and 22 February 1952 all carry items relevant to the Short Shetland.

Index